Grasswork Development Services
E-301 Cloverdale Apartments,
South Main Road,
Koregaon Park, Pune 411001,
India

First published in 2009 by Grasswork Books,
the books unit of Grasswork Development Services

ISBN 978-81-88878-04-8

Typeset in Palatino

Printed in India by
Mudra,
383, Narayan Peth,
Pune 411030, India
mudraoffset@gmail.com

Curious Companions
Ireland to India by Bicycle

Written and Illustrated by

Jake Bullough

Grasswork Books

Dedication

For Sue, Pete, Randhir, Gitti and Sam without whose continuous support and encouragement, my ambitions would never become reality.

Contents

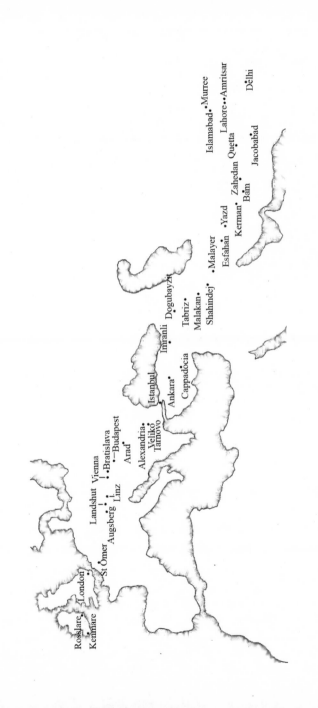

Rosslare
Kenmare
London
St Omer
Augsberg
Landshut Vienna
Linz
Bratislava
Budapest
Arad
Alexandria
Veliko
Tarnovo
Istanbul
Ankara
Cappadocia
Imranli
Dogubayzit
Tabriz
Malakan
Shahindej
Malayer
Esfahan
Yazd
Kerman
Bam
Zahedan
Quetta
Jacobabad
Islamabad
Murree
Lahore
Amritsar
Delhi

Introduction

To explore the world is a passion that consumes many lives, an obsession one is powerless to control. To deny it increases its attraction, to embrace it breeds one's love all the more.

I was blessed with such an affliction from an early age. I had no choice but to face an ambition that would challenge me, both physically and mentally, more than anything I had previously undertaken. The thought had been there for years but reservations had always condemned it to the depths of impracticality. Cycling from my home in the peaceful countryside of Kerry, Ireland, to the untamed metropolis of New Delhi, India, would commit me to testing the limits of my endurance and strength of will.

People asked me, 'Why would you do something so gruelling? What inspires you to do such things? Oh! But why?' The inspiration for my travelling began with my mother but was driven by the words of Ireland's greatest ever adventurer, Dervla Murphy, the epitome of Irish humility. It was during the winter of 1963 that Ms Murphy's dream of cycling from Ireland to India was realised and forty five years later this dream still inspires the world's craving for understanding and exploration. To strive to reach the heights of her extraordinary writing talents would be foolish but I hope my efforts do bring at least muted pleasure to those who still care a little for the permissive, uncouth youth of today.

Tolerance and the condemnation of preconceived stereotypes is where my actions originate. To approach every new person as an individual without comparisons, all new situations without fears or preconceptions, each new day as a chance to live my dream, is simply how I learn. I try to live life by my own rhythm while seeking out the positive for surely wasting time is a sin.

Spontaneity, I believe, is paramount to an adventure. To plan and organize creates expectations. Expectations manifest anxiety and disappointment. Spontaneity dissolves expectations. To be free of expectations is to experience without prejudice.

The planning and preparation for the trip was intentionally minimal and I set off at the end of December with myriad emotions competing for supremacy. Apprehension I know is only natural when confronting the unknown, yet by being unperturbed you cannot help but become exhilarated by your own daring. To shun an experience because of fear is a fatal flaw that condemns people to a self absorbed, banal life of routine. I dispelled my inhibitions and decided to cycle to India.

1

Familiar Territory,
Unfamiliar People

As I crossed the familiar damp and misty countryside of the south coast of Ireland a barrage of ambiguous questions kept my mind occupied. Am I being selfish by once again taking off on a trip when I ought to be planning a stable future like the vast majority of my friends? I have already taken a year out for nine consecutive years. Is it not time to see the bank manager about a hundred and ten percent mortgage which will bring me my dream home along with thirty five years of commitment? Should I not now have planned, after so much fanciful experimentation, my exact career path? I have to admit that I am not getting any younger and although people often tell me how young I am, I am no longer as young as I used to be. Should I not at least have a serious girlfriend as proof of my worth since puberty? No to all of the above thank you very much.

The patter of rain kept me company as I set the tent up in wasteland overlooking a swollen river near Macroom. It was New Year's Eve. I quietly drank pints as the town mourned the death of a local eighteen year old who had taken his own life. The tragedy was a sobering reminder of how important it is to live my life the way that makes me happy and not in order to fulfil the expectations of family, friends or society in general. I agonised over what had driven this young man to want to escape his life so desperately.

The atmosphere was sombre as people diligently drank away their sorrows.

'What do ya think of the Christmas lights on the street they're then young man?' A docile old man with a bushy grey beard asked me.

'They're alright,' I mumbled half-heartedly.

'They are a total waste of electricity if ya ask me boy.'

'I guess your right.' I actually thought they looked kind of drab.

An Italian couple struggled to order a half pint.

'Have ya seen those dirty Romanians in the city?' He whispered as a frown overcame his face. 'They are dirty feckers them refugees. They come here begging for money. Shur they are rich already. They think we are fools boy. I'd be out in the fields most days but I'd be worried them tinkers would come into town looking to rob the clothes off your back if ya weren't looking like.' He took a large swig and ordered us another round.

My misguided compatriot obviously lived a very sheltered existence and became insecure and defensive when confronted with issues that questioned his comfortable life. He had labelled all asylum seekers 'Romanians' thus, in his mind, not to be trusted gypsies. He was oblivious of these people's desperation. He cared little that their lives may have been in danger in their homelands, that they anguished over not being able to provide for their families or that they prayed for the day they would be allowed work an honest job in this country. Although I did sympathise with his insecurity, his narrow minded drone of assumed misgivings was all too familiar.

After several minutes, our attempted football conversation fell flat. Even our Kerry-Cork rivalry was tedious.

'What is your opinion on the strict *purdah* segregation in Islamic societies?' I asked, feigning seriousness, enjoying the confusion that inevitably ensued before explaining my question in simpler terms.

'Oh them fellas lock their women up don't they. They could teach the young ones around here a thing or two, I tell ya.' He stared longingly at the slender legs of a girl who sauntered by wearing a miniskirt. I finished my pint, snuck into my sodden tent and fell asleep cradling a half-eaten chicken burger.

The sound of boy racers screeching around the road, recklessly in search of attention, woke me from strange dreams. Crows squawked as I loaded the bike, reminding me of my old commerce teacher. I shivered at the thought of school. Villages decorated in flickering Christmas lights, quietly suffered from the previous night's exertions. At a petrol station I fought off the contemptuous attentions of a group of guys who mocked my scruffy clothes and left me to battle with my own feelings of intolerance.

I cruised around Cork City before dropping into a betting shop to shout at a TV and lose money. Horse racing was nothing more to me than an excuse to curse and a way to break the day's monotony.

Towards Rosslare, potholes jolted my apprehension into life and impatient traffic condemned my positive demeanour to a long gone era. On reaching the port, I lay shivering in my tent and wallowed in self pity. The previous day's struggles had taken their toll. My asthma had steadily worsened, leaving me gasping for breath and detesting the ice cold air which exasperated the pain in my chest. I rubbed arnica cream onto my aching hamstring and throbbing knee but couldn't help thinking that I may as well have peed on my leg for all the good it did. I leaned out the zip door to vomit and collapsed on the frosted grass, weak from a protesting stomach. I felt miserable. Maybe I deserved to be.

I was mentally prepared for the challenges I would encounter but to be hit so soon with such severe physical problems and the thought of not even making it out of the country, sent waves of humiliation convulsing through my mind. I had talked of a trip that would take me half way around the world and to fail there on my doorstep was utterly inconceivable.

After a sleepless night I bound out of the ice covered tent determined that things would improve. Gentlemen walked their dogs as I jogged around the sand-dunes like a delinquent, still cocooned in my sleeping bag, trying to regain the circulation in my frozen body before boarding the 'Isle of Inishmore' ferry.

On disembarking I faced a bombardment of large hail stones and decided that a visit to the local Welsh hospital and two days of recovery were in order. The compassionate but peculiar doctor wore his trousers up around his chest and his hair tightly gelled to his scalp. He was sympathetic and I gratefully accepted the antibiotics he prescribed free of charge. The storm tapped on the window pane of my cupboard-sized room above a noisy bar and I chastised my body for being so vulnerable.

Even though the Welsh countryside was overcome by the onslaught of winter, I gazed contentedly at the scenes I passed. Dark naked trees silhouetted against the sky, flocks of sheep huddled together in crisp white fields and kids slid excitedly about on frozen ponds. A cosy café in St Clear tempted me inside and I chatted to the three bored waitresses while I sipped coffee and thawed my feet. As I explained my intentions for the coming months the girls looked at me sceptically, thinking I was in search of admiration. They couldn't believe the fact that I had cycled from South West Ireland and the thought of even reaching London was insanity to them. Their lives were dominated by Full English Breakfasts, holidays in Tenerife, TV soaps and drunken nights out. No doubt these things have their place in life but all too often they sadly become the only focus of people's lives.

That night I found myself searching in vain for a Bed and Breakfast in the midst of a dark invisible moor. My headlamp illuminated the deluge before me and water trickled down my grimacing face. The road was a steep incline and as I stood on the greasy pedals my foot slipped, thrusting my hips forward and crunching my crotch into the handlebars. I toppled over in agony and lay in the foetal position surrounded by darkness, feeling the torrent of water rush over my

Curious Companions

sweating body. Thoroughly soaked and exhausted, I was left with no choice but to bunk down in a hay barn. I began to seriously regret my decision to abandon the tent and stay in cheap hotels, hostels and people's houses, wherever possible, as it would not only be beneficial for my health but also add to the adventure. That night, however, I crawled into my sleeping bag, covered it in straw and felt oddly comforted by my modest lodgings.

The moor was stained shades of brown, ochre, pale greens and yellows in the morning light. Sheep and horses roamed freely amongst heather and cotton grass. Passing through the rolling hills of Gloucester and Cheltenham I admired the unhurried way of quaint villages. Enormous bulls strutted about, proudly sporting shining nose rings and a magnificent white horse galloped alongside me down a tranquil back lane. At a beautifully preserved thatched cottage displaying local art work, I sipped tea with a bus load of wacky old age pensioners.

'Oh golly gosh, how extraordinary and marvellous!' They exclaimed having interrogated me about my activities, making me blush. I left with a barrage of 'Cheerio,' and 'Toodaloo,' ringing in my ears.

Oxford's ancient architecture did not disappoint nor did the sight of all the gorgeous female students. I revelled in the university atmosphere for two days, contemplating my life's direction. I yearned to join UK's most revered students in their quest for educational excellence but instead washed my smelly clothes and cycled into the rain. Life is all about priorities.

My knees had ceased to cause me problems, I could breath without wincing in pain and I now covered my daily average one hundred and twenty kilometres without any great difficulty. However, negotiating the labyrinth of streets into the centre of London provided a new set of challenges.

My first adviser was an extremely hairy man in his thirties. He had noticed the Irish flag dangling from my handlebars and introduced himself as being 'in love' with an Irish woman. Lover boy was on his way to work as an emergency medic, a career I stand in high regard. His tight cycling shorts left little to the imagination and his lanky frame bent uncomfortably over his undersized bike. I received an impromptu invitation to his wedding before he directed me into a tunnel forbidden to cyclists.

I had become incredibly lost, regretting the decision to listen to the directions given by a homeless man with socks on his hands. We sat together under a walkway as he mocked the welldressed businessmen who marched friskily by. Emilio was his adopted name, having discarded his original along with his past. His strong cockney accent was incomprehensible at times, especially as his scared mouth often seemed to have a mind of its own. His trembling yellow stained hand clutched a flimsy rolled cigarette and he made me laugh with his imitation of the Queen.

He swore me to confidence before divulging the secrets of living homeless in London, boasting of a place where he went to sit in sparkling Mercedes while their owners fattened themselves at an overpriced restaurant. He received daily invites to attend parties and often found himself getting stoned amongst the city's affluent. He revelled in being used for people's weekly acts of goodwill, an opportunity to rid themselves of any guilt related to the privileged materialistic lives they live.

Although in poor health he enjoyed his life and wouldn't have changed it for any of the creature comforts we all clutter our lives with. He was desperate to prevent me from leaving. Smiling broadly he informed me that it was nearly after work drinks hour, when he pretended to beg outside fancy bars and eateries but actually went to ogle beautiful women. He supposedly knew the best spots but no matter how tempting it was to sit on the pavement and be Emilio's perv buddy, I wished him farewell.

Everyone I asked was adamant the tube was the only human way possible to cross the city and I could see their point as I nearly got arrested for cruising down a motorway gleefully ignoring the protesting traffic. A little bit of Irish charm goes a long way and I received yet another invitation, this time to the birthday party of a policeman, which I politely yet sternly declined.

I took full advantage of my aunt's hospitality and spent two gloriously uneventful days lying on a couch watching TV, drying out and fattening myself on pints of Guinness and Steak and Kidney pies.

Leaving was almost as difficult as entering this metropolis as I sank deep in murky puddles, laughed shamelessly as trucks sent waves lapping at my sides and deafening me with blasts of their war crying horns.

On reaching Taversham, I searched by streetlight for somewhere to stay and was eventually directed to a dilapidated council house owned by a delightfully eccentric old lady. The house was surrounded by old washing machines, pots of wilted plants, discarded Christmas decorations, a large pile of rotting shoes and an old rusting VW van. A caravan covered in wild vines had its wheels replaced by concrete blocks and plastic sheeting flapped desperately on its roof. Following the seventy year old up the spiral staircase I diverted my eyes from her absurdly short skirt and admired the assortment of ornaments and souvenirs that adorned every inch of wall, shelf and floor space. Elongated wooden giraffes looked shyly upon glass frogs covered with thick dust and a Spiderman plaque hung proudly next to a painting of an African tribe.

Doris's matted hair protruded at the most absurd angles and her cackle of a laugh was unnerving. She urged me to use the 'modern' kitchen but piles of mouldy pots and plates proved to be a slight hindrance. I attempted to take a shower but fragments of fluorescent green paint clogged the cracked bath's plug hole. Cats lurked in dark corners, dogs scratched from behind locked doors and I felt I would have been far safer staying at the nearby zoo.

The crashing sound of lamps and books being flung violently about in the next room woke me. The Eastern European occupants were seemingly at war and shouted rather amusing abuse at each other while simultaneously destroying their belongings.

The sun shone brightly on my face as I pedalled into the crisp morning in a jovial mood. On the dual carriageway, several kilometres before Dover, I was startled by the squeal of tyres not far behind me.

Curious Companions

Turning my head I saw a car sliding sideways in my direction before it thankfully gripped the slippery surface several metres behind me and dramatically spun around facing the oncoming traffic. The driver was a thoroughly shaken man from Birmingham who apologized profusely and cursed the lack of visibility in the morning's dazzling sun.

Or reaching Dover port, I watched sea gulls soar and glide over the white cliffs and chatted to a retired fisherman being walked by his hyperactive dog. His granddaughter was strapped to his back, swathed in woolen blankets resembling a baby Eskimo, a tear perched on a smooth chubby cheek.

As the ferry pulled away I desperately tried to recapture my pathetic command of the French language. I wished for the first time that I had not been such a stubborn teenager, blatantly refusing for so many years to learn from my intolerable French teacher.

St. Omer was my first night's stop and I nervously negotiated for a room in a *Chambre D'Hote*. The large smiling lady understood nothing of my muddled mix of Spanish, Irish and occasional French words. No matter how many times I repeated the lines in my head beforehand the resulting noise was incomprehensible and repulsive. 'Si vous plait an bhfuil una habitation por un duine amhain para une nuit agat, ahh gracias beaucoup.' Needless to say languages have never been my forte.

The lady led me reassuringly by the arm to a large luxurious double room where I tiptoed about apologetically dripping muddy rainwater on her plush carpets. I ventured out for a beer but found my anxiety about talking dampen my mood so sat sulking in the corner of a bar, jealous of the ease with which people spoke their beautiful language.

On the road again, I frequently stopped for breaks in charming cafés where gentle old men wearing berets greeted one another with affectionate kisses, I felt a tint of envy at their close comradeship. No sign of machismo here but apparent unconditional goodwill. I drank strong espresso and watched irate women play TV bingo.

Nearby was a huge burial ground of fallen troops from World War II. I studied the white headstones of young men from all over the world who had died tragically fighting for a freedom which we in Europe take for granted today. I sat at the base of a memorial contemplating the waste and fragility of life.

I sheltered from the rain at a grave dedicated to Czech troops who died fighting in this lonely farmland that extended as far as the eye could see. It was a haunting place with plastic flowers scattered haphazardly about and I played my *tin whistle* hoping it may comfort the souls of those who died in this alien land. I had previously visited the solemn sights of Utah and Omaha beaches in Normandy, but that day had been unprepared for such morbid sights.

Almost immune to the endless memorials, spiralling white-faced graveyards, overgrown military barracks and concrete bunkers, my mind strayed to advent calendars, pop tarts and the Aran Islands. As night fell I stopped at a trench set in a forest that looked down across the valley and supposedly any attacking forces. The inside of the bunker was reinforced with corrugated iron and coarse graffiti decorated the water-stained walls. Lying in my sleeping bag on the concrete floor, I drifted to sleep listening to the sounds of the forest and imagining the echo of gunfire.

The weather deteriorated for several days until I found myself caught in a ferocious storm. The wind swept uninterrupted across the open plains and molested me with absolute disregard for my wellbeing. Ice cold rain slapped my face and ripped at my hopelessly ineffective rain jacket. Huge lorries thundered past only inches from my handlebars, leaving me grunting and groaning like a struggling tennis player, as I desperately tried to control my uncooperative bike. I leaned at such an absurd angle against the uncompromising wind that on several occasions it literally blew the bike from under me, depositing me helplessly in a tangled heap. I lay gazing up at the threatening sky, the muddy water of the ditch enveloping me and laughed at what an insane sight I must have been. I waved to bewildered passersby looking from misty car windows with a mixture of wonder and apprehension.

Curious Companions

I hadn't stopped to eat all day as I couldn't feel my hands from the cold but eventually knocked timidly on the door of a tiny thatched house and asked for some drinking water. Although a little surprised by the bedraggled foreigner standing before him, the kind man ushered me inside. The room was scantily furnished and clothes hung drying in the corner. I stood by the wood fire awkwardly reciting platitudes, Holy Mary peered down from a wooden beam and a pair of worn slippers warmed on a neatly stacked pile of firewood. Jean had a weathered yet healthy face and wore a humble green cardigan peppered with holes.

His wife urged me somewhat forcibly to discard my saturated clothes. I sat feeling self-conscious in my tight contour-hugging long johns, looking like a dejected ballerina, while Mrs Jean stood over me caressing my hair with a towel as coarse as sandpaper. The sensual feeling of a head massage is something I regard as universally pleasurable, no matter who the hidden provider may be. Therefore, with my eyes closed, I suddenly realised I had inadvertently become semi aroused. I quickly counted backwards, thought of anything remotely unattractive and off-putting while trying desperately to cover up my indiscretion. Jean made small talk as his frisky wife rubbed harder and faster seemingly enjoying herself. Her sweet suggestively erotic voice whispered in my ear and I gripped the chair fearfully. I imagined all the possible disastrous outcomes and damage to international relations. After an eternity of discomfort I escaped her clutches, hunched over faking a stomach ache to a couch nearby. I grabbed the only thing within reach for cover and felt bad for the confused napping cat. Embarrassment avoided, I felt indebted to this most generous couple and spent the evening curled up on the cosy sofa listening to traditional French folk music from an antique radio.

As the days unfolded I passed through near-deserted villages, their residents evading the bad weather by staying indoors behind firmly locked shutters. The streets looked ugly without people and the whistle and whine of the wind was sinister. The only signs of life were puffing chimneys, echoes of barking dogs and silently circling sea gulls.

My bike developed its first defects and I spent the night at a small guesthouse near the German border owned by a friendly lady and her excitable nun sister, while a car mechanic cheerfully hammered away with total disdain for my machine. The sister was obviously unused to having male guests and on shaking my hand felt compelled to stroke my arm with her quivering fingers. She had a nervous twitch, blinked uncontrollably and I couldn't help but feel uneasy especially on noticing the long whiskers protruding from her face. The view of the car park was an uninspiring mess of shopping trolleys and burnt out cars. Sheets of rain struck blinking streetlamps and car headlights reflected in a pond decorated with floating crisp packets.

In a café I admired an ancient unresponsive gentleman who sat beneath a poster of a voluptuous blonde in a frilly Bavarian outfit, proudly displaying her giant assets and evidently advertising a Belgian beer perched between.

While having my morning shower I opened my soapy eyes to see the sister standing in her white habit in the doorway, eyes aglaze and mouth open. I'm not one to stifle a woman's curiosity so stood unashamedly exposed and wished her a polite 'bonjour'. She pretended to rearrange the towels for some time with eyes fixed on me before skipping merrily out the door.

Passing into Germany I occupied myself by trying to pronounce place names like Schwindratzheim and Schwarwaldhoftstrabe. Huge beautifully preserved wooden Bavarian houses lined the streets. It was an astonishing fifteen degrees and I cycled in a t-shirt. I paused at the brown muddy slopes of a ski field as the sun shone through the clouds for the first time since I left England. Bored tourists sunbathed on blankets, their skis lying dormant on the roof of their cars. I had expected extreme cold and snow in Germany and now found myself

Curious Companions

oddly disappointed. The sky turned to spectacular pinks, oranges and purples as I rocketed downhill through dense forest. The Stereophonics blasted in my ears and I felt elated after an extremely satisfying day.

Well maintained cycle paths snaked their way through the countryside, their direction often defying logic, climbing a hillock only to bizarrely double back on themselves without warning. I carried the bike through ankle-deep muddy fields back to the main road and let roar every German swear-word in my vocabulary, frightening crows into flight. I became infuriatingly lost and decided the Germans do have a sense of humour after all.

Flash BMWs and Mercedes sped by at hair-raising speed. I puffed my way patiently forward, boredom beginning to take its toll. Bizarrely I found the constant presence of truck wheels within inches of my face almost comforting and I had to fight off the urge to reach out and embrace them.

One day while lying in a field eating the last of my repulsively blackened bananas, a stooped old man appeared by my side. He used a smooth cane to feel his way and squinted at me as if nearly blind. His ancient duffel coat and fur hat perfectly suited his persona.

Unsure where I was going to spend the night I enquired about a hotel. He began to chuckle, then to cough and choke. I helped him back to his miniature hut hidden behind a clump of orange trees. Having recovered sufficiently he proceeded to prepare tea, placing a blackened pot over a small coal cooker. I attempted conversation but my efforts were pointless as we shared only about ten words in common. He had a delicate cough when he talked. The only picture he owned was of a crucifix which hung mouldy over his bed. We sat in tranquil silence listening to the crackle of the fire.

He gave up on the tea with a flurry of abuse and rattled around in a cardboard box under the bed, proudly producing a bottle of whisky. We drank it straight, me using his one and only green chipped mug and him swigging happily from the bottle. I wondered about his family and past and felt both affection and pity for the old man. His bright eyes shone behind a cracked, tired looking face, no doubt the consequence of a long arduous life.

My grandfather would have been about the same age as him, had he still been alive. It fascinated me that they could have fought opposite each other in the Second World War and the consequences of such an encounter on both our lives. This reclusive yet jovial gentleman who sat before me would have once been labelled the enemy, causing me once again to detest the tragedy of war.

With his faithful dog curled up around my feet I played a few tunes. My host closed his eyes, reclined on the bed and swayed with the rhythm of the slow airs. He bounced up and down excitedly on the springy mattress as I attempted faster jigs and reels. He giggled as whisky dribbled down his unshaven chin, a huge smile revealing toothless gums. He clapped his little wrinkled hands to the beat, the dog howled and I found myself in the most unexpected, yet intimate and enjoyable experience of the trip thus far.

Curious Companions

2

Fights and Frolics

The exceptionally friendly receptionist at the Augsburg Youth Hostel was a welcome change from the obnoxious oafs I habitually had to deal with. I wondered then why I automatically assumed he was gay.

I used the internet and couldn't prevent myself from glancing past my monitor at an attractive girl in her late teens. Her long glossy black hair fell over bare shoulders and a large hat hid her face. To my surprise her low cut top became progressively inadequate at covering her cleavage. She was entertaining someone via a web-cam and also revelled in the startled looks that I failed to conceal. She lowered her top momentarily, a nipple absconded as she giggled at her own daring. Although not complaining at the time, I was stunned at seeing this attractive young woman resort to this somewhat bold behaviour.

The illuminated cathedral dominated the huge central square and I lounged in a café watching snowflakes sprinkle couples walking hand in hand.

The next day I negotiated frozen puddles and passed by two old age pensioners clutching onto each other for added warmth and happily humming a tune. A little further on, a lone man shuffled down a shaded avenue, his eyes exuding loneliness. I mused over how relationships are more important in one's later life than in the years of hectic careers when people obsess over their possessions.

At a bus stop a little old lady wearing a flowery dress talked to me in German. It wasn't until I had emptied my water bottle that I discovered this sweet looking grandmother was downright insane. She seized the bottle and began whacking me over the head with it. I backed away.

The scene was entertaining for the various onlookers waiting for their bus, unconcerned about coming to my aid. My grey haired attacker screeched abuse, condemning me to whatever hell her demented brain led her to believe in. She jumped up and down, swung the bottle wildly over her head and licked her heavily lipsticked lips, leaving her looking as if she had just parted from a passionate embrace. She picked up plastic wrappers and thin pieces of cardboard packaging and threw them at me only for the wind to blow them back in her face. I stood several metres away unsure how to retrieve my bike without manhandling the old dame, when the bus driver arrived and ushered her safely away. I waved goodbye and received the finger in return.

In Landshut, I checked into an enormous empty hostel overlooking the city's flickering lights. The main cobbled street was lined with multicoloured pastel buildings and I asked a tall, mop-headed young man for directions to the Irish bar, having had cravings for a pint of Guinness all week. He offered to guide me there and then invited himself to join me for a drink.

Randolf was a trainee in a nearby bookshop and although polite, was utterly devoid of personality. I chatted to the barman while my new acquaintance scowled at his pint, disgusted by the taste. I finished both without hesitation and ordered another round.

We visited his bookshop where he showed me his favourite book based on a cartoon character resembling Hitler. To escape his tour of dullness I suggested coffee which I knew he hated. I hoped he would get the hint and disappear but instead condemned me to be his new best friend. Randolf shifted about nervously on a stool like an impatient child, unable to decide on a comfortable position for his long limbs and clumsily scooped hot chocolate from his glass. He fumbled with his shirt sleeves and picked at a scab on his arm. His head tilted to the

Curious Companions

side as he wiped frizzy hair out of his eyes only for it to fall back into place.

For lack of conversation I encouraged him to talk to two stunning women who sipped wine nearby. They were incredibly attractive and totally out of both our leagues but much to my amazement and delight my uncoordinated comrade swooped on their table without hesitation. We spent a thoroughly enjoyable evening together drinking numerous bottles of Pinot Noir. They were both professional models and I liked their honesty and colourful outlooks on life. They were apparently enamoured by our scruffy appearance and youthful charm. I chose to forget that I was in fact older than both. They invited us to visit them next time we were in Berlin. Randolf was indeed my new best friend.

Safety had been a prominent topic of conversation thus far on my trip but I had shrugged it off in order to remain positive. I don't necessarily believe in the Buddhist concept of Karma but I recognize it as an excellent guide on how to act towards fellow human beings. It was on this topic that I had spent the evening writing in a snug café in Linz, Austria. I felt alone in this strange city and wanted to talk to someone but lack of confidence and language prevented me.

Street performers sought the attention of passersby, a hot dog stand did swift business off people walking their dogs and taxi drivers waited patiently for their next fare. I stood on a corner gazing at the cathedral's illuminated spire when a hand was placed on my shoulder.

A volley of incomprehensible German was uttered in a loud whisper and a hard object was forced into the hollow of my back. I felt strangely amused as I could not understand one word of this outburst. I conjured up the mental image of me standing petrified with arms held high in total submission and felt humiliated. A hand clamped tight onto my jacket and a hairy arm reached to relieve me of my camera. I decided that I was in no mood to surrender my valuables and consequently the trip.

I thrust my right elbow back with as much force as I could muster and felt instant agony. My opponent toppled to the ground in an untidy heap. I felt lost, unsure of what to do next. To run was a temptation but somewhat uncharacteristically I found myself determined to defend my pride.

My body lunged forward. I gripped his throat, fingers digging into soft flesh. His head struck the cobblestones, a satisfying thud. I stared into his blue eyes, our grimacing faces only centimetres apart. Warm blood trickled onto my hands. There was a deafening silence as I grasped the screw driver that lay discarded next to me. My mind reeled in rage, resentful of the position I had been forced into. Struggling with conflicting urges, I placed the head of the weapon against his unshaven cheek, yearning to inflict as much pain as was humanly possible, seeking redemption for all the times I had been robbed in the past. Hatred prevailed over my usual preference for restraint as I twisted the tool into my screaming adversary's skin. I snarled insults and demanded an explanation for his cowardly act. My hand closed tightly around his windpipe. I wanted him to re-evaluate his life. I wanted him to remember his callous actions. I wanted him to remember me. I was shocked at the ease with which I inflicted pain.

He whimpered and held my leg loosely as if pleading for mercy. I recovered my self-control. As I backed away he spat a glob of bloodied saliva on my jeans. The loathing he possessed was unnerving. I took a step forward and planted the sole of my right shoe squarely into his pock marked and bloodied face. His nose crunched under the force. He lay still in a pool of blood, his shiny leather jacket spattered with red and a small gold cross dangling awkwardly from his neck.

I stared in disbelief at what I'd done and began to worry about the implications. Was this apparent cruelty I had just displayed justifiable as self-defence, or would the police see it differently? I rang the doorbells of several nearby apartments in the hope someone would find his body and get him to hospital. I remember little about the walk back to the hostel except the throbbing pain in my elbow and the paranoia of police lurking around every dark corner.

Curious Companions

Entering the shower I watched the blood stained water form intricate patterns around my feet. My mind repeated the events of the past traumatic hour, distraught and in search of a logical explanation. Had I subconsciously enjoyed inflicting pain on another human being? Should I have relinquished my camera? Was its value really worth the consequences? I had escaped relatively unharmed with only a swollen arm and insignificant scratches but my heart raced and my hands trembled. I pictured the man's disfigured face, the police out in search of the culprit and the repercussions it might have on the trip.

Leaving early the following morning I cycled precariously past miles of dilapidated factories and power stations pumping out enormous columns of dark smoke. I gripped the handlebars with my left hand and winced in agony with every jolt in the road. The path followed the Danube as it looped its way sluggishly through misty hillsides. I ate lunch admiring swans gliding gracefully on the still surface. Huge sheets of ice drifted languidly along, fishermen stood alone enjoying the tranquillity at sunset.

I pushed the bike over black-iced pavements to a St Polten hostel, tormented by my throbbing arm. The comically ignorant receptionist huffed and sighed as I enquired about a room. She threw a key on the desk and ordered me to report along with my bedclothes for breakfast at seven thirty. I lay on my bed staring at the ceiling as my roommate, a courteous trainee chef, talked sweet nothings to his girlfriend on the phone for two hours.

Unable to sleep I ventured down to the cafeteria where I sat in a daze surrounded by a mob of energetic young teenagers on a school tour. They eyed me quizzically. Two girls were significantly taller than their classmates and wore short skirts and make-up, in an obvious attempt to look older. They huddled together and whispered excitedly. I attempted to write but my brain refused to respond.

The two girls approached and asked me with cheeky grins if I would buy them alcohol. I dismissed their request outright but this only fuelled their audacity. They told me they drank every weekend at parties held by their elder male friends and invited me to their room where we would apparently be more comfortable. They giggled and I also had to laugh at the bravado of such young girls. I stood up to leave as one began to slide up her skirt provocatively and the other grabbed my backside, I retreated to my room feeling abused and a little foolish.

The act of paedophilia revolts me and even though my sexual deprivation was at an all time high, I did not for one second applaud these rebellious girls' behaviour. They were unashamedly curious and I feared for them, knowing there a 'e limitless guys who would willingly exploit their naivety.

I often became hypnotized by the infinite metre-long white lines disappearing underneath me. I forgot to look up for long periods and suddenly noticed that the surrounding countryside had dramatically changed. Endless fields, uniformly ploughed and awaiting the arrival of spring, were replaced by a scattering of plain uninspiring white houses. Then came an enchanting forest bustling with wildlife and next a peaceful village.

I was amazed at how well my body was coping with the pressures of cycling up to ten hours a day. My legs felt strong and my energy levels high. Apart from my elbow, my only worry was that for the past week I had been coughing up blood in the mornings which probably should have concerned me more than it did.

One evening saw me following a frozen dirt track along a reservoir, not knowing nor caring where it may lead. Large flocks of birds filled the sky before coming to rest in a flourish on a small island. It was bitterly cold but I succumbed to the temptation to spend the night in my new tranquil world. I found a dilapidated restaurant that catered to picnicking summer tourists and squeezed my way inside through a smashed window. A thick layer of dust covered the stacked tables and chairs. For lack of anything else to stem my hunger I chanced an out of date can of cold baked beans. The place was a little eerie with cobwebs decorating the ceiling and rustling vermin in dark corners, yet I slept soundly on a rickety table.

Curious Companions

I awoke early to splendid silence and a mouse playing house with my shoe. The lake was glass, mirroring the trees on the far bank and I felt guilty for dipping my toe in, disturbing the flawless surface. I sat on the veranda playing my whistle, shattering the peace. Ducks came to investigate the early morning commotion.

Later that day I cycled along in bright sunshine but could not rid myself of a foul mood. I often try to figure out why I sometimes become annoyed with life but am still at a loss. I decided on a break in a simple café and chatted to a waitress with the most delightfully cheerful demeanour. Her stylishly straightened hair had blonde streaks from a bottle and her face radiated happiness. The fumbling awkwardness of her movements made her all the more attractive. She treated me to cakes and we chatted with surprising ease. I mumbled gratitudes and embarrassed us both with a corny chat-up line before leaving with her email address in my pocket and a wide smile on my face.

It's amazing the difference a little company can make to one's disposition and for the rest of the day I felt as if I hadn't a care in the world. It's also miraculous the effect the mind has on the body and I whizzed along as if magically propelled.

I arrived in Vienna city centre amidst a deluge of hail and sleet. Cloaked women in doorways refused to give me directions as ice bounced off my face. The backpacker hostel reception area was littered with posing American snowboarders and I felt peculiar being back amongst English speakers. I shared my room with two South African girls who I couldn't understand.

Vienna has always conjured up romantic images for me as Paris does for most people. I pictured myself strolling along cobbled streets hand in hand with a beautiful woman, gazing at the architecture and enjoying the atmosphere of café terraces. However, reality was somewhat different. I spent my first evening watching football and drinking beer in a murky bar along with a boisterous crowd of mostly foreign male immigrants. I enjoyed watching their distinctive mannerisms.

A table of three Chinese men sipped their beers, fidgeted restlessly and lost interest in the football. They watched a screen showing ski shooting and became hugely animated. Turkish guys talked non-stop about football and ordered a pizza to share, speaking patronizingly to the waiter as if they were doing him a favour. They sipped tea and eyed the passing clientele with suspicion. A lone African man hogged an entire table only relenting to the company of a shy black man who had clung to the back wall. He shouted indignantly at the television in frustration and received no response from his silent companion. He stretched his legs out with total disregard for passersby and hissed to gain the waiter's attention. Two young Indians in smart suits looked like regulars to this seedy sports betting hall. A lone man with wild grey hair sat at a chaotic table piled high with newspapers, an overflowing ashtray, half empty coffee mugs and brandy tumblers with his dog asleep at his feet. He was enveloped in thick cigar smoke and meticulously filled out a football coupon without ever removing his sunglasses.

The weather had transformed itself the next day and I strode along with my newly acquired tourist map happy to mingle with the city's international clientele. Tour groups, concert ticket sellers and art students danced around one another in the streets. Young and old alike enjoyed the city's vibrancy. I gorged myself on chocolate truffles, perfectly presented coffee and immersed myself unreservedly in the institutional cafés. Art galleries, book shops and antique stores lined the avenues. I sat in a shaded corner of Stephansplatz and admired the ancient tiled roofs and tall slender tower of the Gothic St. Stephen's Cathedral juxtaposed by ultra modern chic hotels with innovative glass exteriors.

Slight apprehension clouded my mind as I crossed into Slovakia. I had negative preconceptions regarding Bratislava but was determined to challenge these as yet unfounded opinions. Large dilapidated tower blocks dominated the skyline on the far bank of the river. The road was quiet and to my surprise the first Slovak I came face to face with was a balaclava clad jogger. Was this an opportunistic mugger loitering near the border in the hope of getting first pickings of the newly arrived tourists? His steely eyes darted to the side as I gripped the bicycle pump in apprehension.

The suburbs were a depressing mix of heavily fortified houses. Along the riverside abandoned concrete dwellings with smashed windows were decorated in elaborate graffiti. On reaching the centre of Bratislava I felt at ease as the quaint cobbled streets were busy with gorgeous women tottering about on high heels, wearing white fur coats and oversized shades. I had never before seen such beauty and became more concerned with my shabby appearance than for my personal safety. A stunning tall blonde, immaculately dressed in a business suit and miniskirt and never ending legs, linked arms with an overweight man wearing a shiny blue tracksuit and a neck bedecked in tattoos. No doubt I was insanely jealous.

The hostel was pleasantly disorganized and I checked into a dorm alongside three Australians. The two guys were overtly camp and seemed determined that the world should stand up and take notice. Their companion was a girl who adored orange. They jumped on a bed, hugging and shouting to the crooning of Enrique Englesias. They were fascinated with my trip and I felt somewhat like a fake celebrity. I awoke that night to the noise of a group of drunken teenagers from Dublin abusing the receptionist before one threw up on the pool table and another pissed in the hallway.

My rest day was unexciting until I met Katya that evening. I was absorbed in my book when from across the café I sensed a pair of eyes watching me intently. They belonged to a girl with shiny dark red hair. The place was busy as waiters rushed about and heavy metal blasted out of the speakers. I could no longer concentrate on reading. Our eyes met several times amidst the commotion. She gave me a warm smile and raised an eyebrow before drifting out into the dark. I sat, my mind in turmoil, undecided whether to follow. Eventually I scrambled out the door, clumsily knocking over the waiter's tray in the process.

Out in the dimly lit street I saw her dark figure lying on the grass of a nearby park. She gazed skywards, smoke slowly drifting from her mouth. I lay down by her side and stared nervously at the branches above, unsure of what I was doing. Drunk men argued, a dog tackled a rubbish bin and I began to worry I'd made a dreadful mistake. Thankfully I felt her hand envelop mine and we lay in a blissful silence. Her hands were cold yet soft and she grinned as I inserted one up my sleeve. I took a drag on her cigarette and spluttered pitifully. She stroked my face tenderly, her long eyelashes flickered and I realized I had already become infatuated.

Words were unnecessary as we skipped through the empty streets holding hands. It felt like such a simple yet significant gesture of affection, conquering all language barriers. We sat on a bridge overlooking a polluted river. I made an attempt at conversation but to my delight she shrugged her shoulders, leaned over placing a finger to my lips and kissed me tenderly. The scent of her perfume lingered. We shivered from a combination of the cool night air and nervousness. We held each other close, she nestled her head in my neck and I marvelled at how I had come to find myself in such a situation.

Suddenly she took my head in her hands, kissed me, jumped off the wall and ran down the dark street. I sat bemused for a few moments, quite sure I would never see this silent mysterious girl again, when a taxi pulled up and inside her beaming face beckoned me. Thoughts of possible kidnapping, robbery and torture competed with those of happiness, exhilaration and desire. We listened to the taxi driver's inane questioning. She blatantly ignored him so I did likewise. She stared out the window as street lights flickered past. She frowned and her lips pursed. She seemed puzzled. She gripped her handbag tightly and I dreaded she was having second thoughts.

Her timid demeanour disappeared when we reached her rundown apartment block. She pushed me violently against a wall and kissed me with erupting passion. Her hands grasped at me urgently and we became lost in a flurry of excitement. Her nails scraped my back, she bit my chest and disposed of my belt in fury. Thoughts of possible danger evaporated with the exquisite pleasure as she dropped to her knees.

After an exhilarating night we lay in the bathtub enveloped in each others arms. A limp flower had discarded its petals onto a glass shelf and scented oils created a false sense of nature. She became alive

Curious Companions

when I touched her. She laughed and I wished I knew why. She stepped daintily from the bath and wrapped a towel around her glistening body, the folds of her back elegant and addictive. I knew that being deaf was not a hindrance for this amazing woman. Nor, I realised, did it interfere with my feelings for her. Leaving would no doubt be the biggest challenge of the trip thus far.

I didn't know too much about Hungary but several days later, I arrived in Budapest cycling along a muddy track lined with abandoned decaying houses and huge slabs of repetitive apartment blocks. I encountered a group of burly workmen loading large logs of a dismembered tree onto a truck. One gentleman with a bulging stomach and flabby arms protruding from his sleeveless shirt, stood out in my path. I nodded my usual 'gutten morgen,' having forgotten what country I was now in and negotiated around him. He hocked up phlegm and spat at me. Luckily he was a bad shot and his projectile landed on the ground at the feet of his bemused associates. Fair enough I looked bizarre but the malice this bad tempered brute showed was demoralizing. Did he see me as some freeloading rich kid who cycled about happily while he broke his back trying to make ends meet? Was his resentment justified and was I in fact flaunting my relatively comfortable background? I always remember a quote from the Dalai Lama which says, 'We can each of us only offer what we have.' I was glad I was able to smile and wave goodbye as this idiot had to live with his needless hatred.

Pausing in the city centre to rest, I scoffed copious amounts of ice cream in a luxurious shopping mall. I had to laugh as two quintessentially English lady tourists sat uncomfortably alongside three large-breasted prostitutes who laughed raucously, proudly displaying their implants for all those inclined to look. A man performed awesome music on a line of glasses filled with varying amounts of water, his face deep in concentration. Frozen old men played chess in the metro as people rushed all around them.

That night I found myself lying under a bridge eating the remnants of a packet of cornflakes with three old alcoholic women and a man with a deformed leg. I'm sure I would have enjoyed the architecture, fine dining and entertainment of the city but felt welcome there. The women bickered over a bottle of cheap vodka and my friend Arnold, showed me newspaper cuttings of celebrities who he was adamant were his family. The women's hair was bizarrely matted and rips in their decaying clothes showed patches of filthy wrinkled skin. Arnold believed I was also homeless, but because I had come from Ireland was somewhat more affluent. I showed him photos of my family and he hugged me close in a repugnant attempt to comfort me over the loss of such a beautiful family. He smelt like a goat. He began to sing a lament which echoed eerily under the bridge, his eyelids half closed. The women fell unconscious, covered in a blanket of cardboard to stem the freezing night air. I dozed off sharing my sleeping bag with my unusual friend who slept with his mouth wide open displaying brown rotten teeth and poisoning me with his toxic breath. I felt simultaneously repulsed by but sympathetic to their pitiful life.

3

Canine Conflict,
Human Conundrum

My thoughts were divided. One minute I enjoyed the rain on my face and the freedom I had to explore but the next I questioned my own sanity for having chosen to undertake such a demanding ordeal. Suddenly an overtaking car lost control, shaking me out of my contemplation. I watched as if in slow motion as it careered along the centre line, smoke discharging from its tyres. The driver fought to control the vehicle in the wet conditions, eventually coming to an abrupt halt in the grassy verge. He was miraculously lucky to have escaped as I had pictured myself dragging injured bodies or worse from a tangled wreckage. I quietly pedalled past the bearded man who sat on the ground with his head between his legs vomiting from the shock. It was the second such incident in three weeks and I decided not to stop to offer my sympathies.

Women wrapped in shawls carried woven baskets, men wearing large fur hats with long fuzzy ear flaps pulled carts laden with firewood along rutted roads. Children gave chase, waving and cheering excitedly as they hurdled over piles of rubbish and rotting dogs. I passed red-lipped prostitutes waiting in the woods, who beckoned me eagerly but I meekly waved back in embarrassment.

The Australians in Bratislava had told me about a website called Couch Surfing which they had used while travelling. The concept being that travellers, tired of staying in expensive and uninspiring hotels, could log onto the site, choose a location they wished to visit and contact a local person willing to donate their couch for the night. It connected like-minded people interested in making friends from other cultures and the idea was that once they returned home they would repay the hospitality to others. I'd decided to give the idea a go, thinking it would be nice to connect with more local people as I pedalled my way through their country.

My first host was a friendly Hungarian by the name of Norbert. His mom welcomed me with outlandish hospitality and his sullen sister with a bemused huff. Norbert was a mine of geographical knowledge and was clear and precise with everything he did and said. His room was choreographed to perfection with medals, posters and books organized as if for a museum display.

We spent the evening with his group of ultra patriotic friends. One mixed a concoction of shots from a variety of homemade liquors, another tested his pain barrier with a stun gun. Their animosity towards their neighbouring countries was sad to see and it surprised me that such grievances still existed. They claimed to have lost over two thirds of their country's territory after the collapse of the Austro-Hungarian Empire and were adamant that one day what was rightfully theirs would be returned. I looked at a map as they pointed out countries like Slovakia, Czech Republic, Slovenia, Bosnia, Poland, Romania, Croatia and Austria who had annexed what was once Hungarian land. One of the guys Attila wanted to cycle the old border and preach the truth to the people who live there. They showed me a Youtube video of journalists being robbed by gypsies in Romania and branded me naive for refusing to buy a gun for protection.

The five of us piled into Juri's beaten up Peugeot and chugged our way into town. We sat with dour friends in a bar lacking atmosphere as everyone stared at the pools of beer and smashed glass on the wooden floor. There was traditional dancing in a back room and I enjoyed watching a guy with a ponytail swing his girlfriend around the floor with great exuberance. We struggled through an hour of billiards, got beaten in table football by two young girls and arrived back home at five a.m. thoroughly exhausted.

I was force-fed breakfast at seven o'clock by Norbert's mother and stopped by Gabor's place where I was plied with more palinja, the local rocket fuel schnapps, by his hilariously boisterous dad. A large group had congregated to see me off and I felt blessed to have met such generous people. I fell off my bike several times that morning due to my state of inebriation.

One day while snacking on cereal in a field, I noticed an elderly lady wallowing in a ditch nearby. The hood of her fluorescent purple and green jacket hung down obscuring her face and two plastic bags dangled from her hand. She shuffled through the long dead grass pulling at a piece of string that held up her tattered trousers. About a metre away she stopped and screwed up her face as if giving birth. I waved a cheery hello but nothing seemed to register. Her face relaxed as I passed her some fruit but she continued to stare through me. She held the banana aloft with scrawny arms as if making a religious offering. Her brow was furrowed and she moved her jaw in a circular motion as if on Ecstasy. Suddenly she dropped to the ground as if released from the force of a magnet and sat cross-legged at my feet munching fervently on the fruit. Half an hour later, after a feast of biscuits and yogurt, she picked up her bags of miscellaneous plastic and metal scraps and hobbled off back to the ditch. She was obviously missing a few marbles and I felt a deep pain at the thought of the difficult life she lived, neglected by society and suffering uncompromising deprivation. I felt foolish as I remounted my expensive bicycle to continue my journey. I often think about that persecuted lady and feel sadness that I could do so little to relieve her misery.

Crossing the border into Romania I was immediately accosted by men who appeared out of the shadows waving wads of notes. Grubby gypsy kids washed car windows and cheered loudly. As I passed yet another ramshackled complex of abandoned cars and dilapidated sheds, a pack of growling dogs darted out of the overgrown verge.

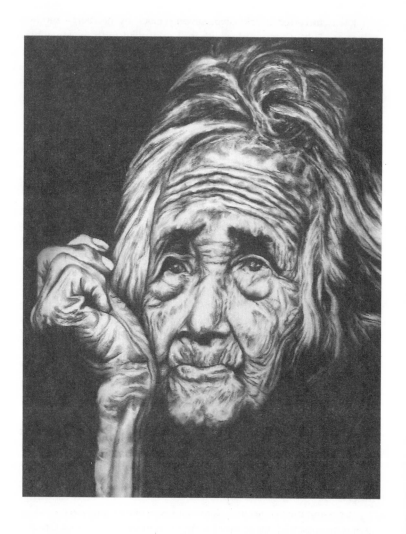

Curious Companions

The leader lunged, I swerved, leaving it skating head first across the tarmac. Another caught up with me barking hysterically, fangs bared. I smacked it firmly between the eyes with my pump and although the loathsome creature was shocked more than hurt, I felt extreme satisfaction seeing it whimper in retreat. I actually quite like dogs but my fondness for my intact body is greater.

The dreary countryside was littered with meadows of plastic rubbish and I saluted old men wrapped in blankets making their way lethargically along on antique carts pulled by equally ancient donkeys.

In Arad that night I was invited to stay in a house with fourteen international volunteers. Some were reticently friendly, others clearly resented my presence. I showered and walked the area with Emmanuelle, a miniature Parisian guy of Indian origin. He spoke broken English and craved an outlet for his frustrations within the house. Questioned about his homeland he pondered for some time before declaring that he believed to originally be from Maharashtra. I told him this was in fact my final destination and he asked me to show him later where it was on a map. I was amazed by his lack of interest in his background and even more when he claimed to detest Asian peoples' 'uncivilized way of life'.

Their building was an impressive luxury three storied villa surrounded by high walls and fronted by a huge ostentatious gate. It resembled a mayor's or a rich business man's residence but was surrounded by sprawling shacks and cheap low-rise apartment blocks. The volunteers had all been sponsored to be there as part of their university studies, most receiving grants from the European Union. This money was given to their respective local volunteer organizations in Arad and they in turn had given these inappropriate lodgings to the students.

What transpired from my conversation with Emmanuelle was that the vast majority of the volunteers were utterly disillusioned, feeling they were merely being used by the program to obtain grant aid. They had gone there with idealistic expectations about helping the 'less fortunate' and were angry at merely being entertained during their stay. They sat about waiting for their daily one hour of English teaching and even that they detested as the kids they taught treated them with contempt. Some of the group refused to teach kids over six as they were apparently 'too difficult', while others told the organization they didn't want to teach at all, so spent their days chatting on the internet. To come to Romania and spend your days selfishly cocooned in a lavish mansion surrounded by poverty was utterly sickening to me and I could then understand why some looked at me with suspicion. Originally wanting to make a difference, these future social workers had ironically become bitter towards the local populace for snubbing their goodwill. They were obviously well intentioned but their presence there was sadly widening the gap that exists between affluent and poor Europe, increasing misunderstandings and spreading resentment.

The house was a hive of protesting youngsters as we arrived back to a meeting between the residents and a representative from a local program. They had made a list of all the problems within the house and I sat in a corner unable to believe what I was hearing. A window latch had been loose for over a month, it took too long for the water to heat up in the downstairs bathroom, the reception on the widescreen television was often fuzzy, never mind the internet connection for the four computers being unavailable some mornings. These spoilt brats sat around on their plush leather couches making lists about trivial inconveniences while people rummaged in refuse bins and lay sleeping on the cold street several metres away.

I craved to escape but instead found myself hypocritically suppressing my opinions in favour of a large plate of pasta. The evening was spent watching cable TV and drowning my prejudices as we greedily consumed over ten bottles of wine. I think this was the program's new tactic to keep the youngsters happy by plying them with cheap alcohol. There were five empty beds in the house that night but I was ordered to sleep on the floor as using a bed whose owner had not given permission, was deemed rude. I felt a little better as the discomfort eased my guilt. I left in the early morning with a sore head and a deep sadness at how people's benevolence can be so incredibly misguided.

Curious Companions

Quarries lined the roadside. I didn't envy the hardworking men coated in black soot. Enormous mounds of broken rock awaited transport and kids played in this harsh playground. Horse and carts plodded along seemingly unaware of the thunderous columns of lorries. I counted an average of seven ten-wheelers to every one car and I thought what a nice job it must be to drive through countries towering over everything and dominating the roads.

An ancient Dacia with a sofa strapped to its roof offered me a lift. I politely declined with a wave of my frozen hand. The houses that edged the road were charming with a central courtyard, mud compacted by generations of feet, areas for pigs, chicken coups and a vegetable garden. A dog lounged in the sun and worn farm tools were propped against wattle and daub walls. Piles of hay stood drying against a central pole and old carts complete with wooden wheels were half filled with freshly cut timber. Large wire drums of corn, the most popular local crop, sat drying. A church was decorated with colourful frescos contrasting the bland monotone countryside. Elaborate biblical scenes looked down upon women wearing black shawls, crouched low washing clothes in frozen streams.

I turned up the classical music on my Ipod to a deafening volume and fantasised about being in a grand Italian concert arena. I imagined sitting alongside the country's most flamboyant women, dressed in ridiculously frilly dresses, and men in tuxedos, complete with cane and top hat. We would listen appreciatively to the performance of a cellist onstage.

'His intonation is flawless in the cruelly high tessitura demanded by the composer,' says my imaginary companion, lighting up a cigar.

'Doesn't his manner simply exude splendour,' articulates his wife while cooling her white painted face with a Chinese fan.

In reality I avoided kamikaze chickens, my ass feeling as if I'd been indecently assaulted the night before, as gold-toothed prostitutes propositioned me with vulgar insinuations.

Two enormous electricity plants bordered the road and puffed vast columns of smoke skyward. My host Elena, bound up to me at the train station with a jolly face and welcomed me so unreservedly that I felt a little uncomfortable with such a public display of affection.

She lived alone in a small one bedroom apartment. I swapped my filthy clothes in favour of merely grubby ones.

Elena urged me to relax on the couch as we became acquainted over a glass of wine. Conversation came easily and she related her parent's days living under Communism. She could not contain her anger and resentment while narrating the years of hardship they endured during Ceausescu controlled Romania. Food was rationed resulting in long hours of standing in queues, fuel and electricity supply was restricted and standards of living had plummeted. Oil and all quality goods were exported to repay international debts. Worst, was the people's constant fear of the Securitate, the secret police, who ensured that any criticism of the regime, or any uprising was immediately suppressed. People had felt hopeless.

Tears came to her eyes as she explained that the most appalling policies were those introduced to increase the population. From 1983 it became the 'duty' of every woman to produce a minimum of five children. Abortion and contraception were abolished and all women in factories subjected to monthly gynaecological examinations. Childless and unmarried women were inflicted with higher taxes and harassment. Orphanages packed with unwanted children and horrific deaths from back street abortions were the result.

She smiled as I took her hand in mine. She told me how people had resorted to religion in rebellion against the regime. It struck me as an ironic contrast to today's youth in Western Europe. Although the conversation was intense we surprised each other with the similarity of our beliefs and ideals.

I genuinely enjoyed her company over those first few hours, although it became apparent that she possessed a large chip on her shoulder. She rightly resented Western Europe for its prejudice, thinking Romania a danger to the Europian Union's integrity. She was also right about Western Europe's generalized opinion of Romania being solely occupied by gypsies – a point reinforced by my friend from Macroom. She detested being considered inferior and although I could sympathize, I felt her bitterness extremely unattractive.

She was obviously very comfortable with her body, my eyes followed her curves around the room and I was pleasantly surprised when she reappeared from the kitchen with her loose zip-down jumper undone to her belly button, inadequately covering her large braless chest. She seemed to have anticipated my weakness for breasts and delighted in my attention as we laughed and flirted with ease. I was feeling bold. We abandoned dinner in favour of a second bottle of wine and that in turn was forgotten in preference for sex. Things had happened fast and spontaneous.

We slept alongside each other as if we had done so for years and not just met a few hours before at the train station. Although I found my bed companion attractive, I would not have pursued her were it not for the flaunting of her tempting body and forward behaviour.

I gazed across the pink sheets at this snoring stranger and mused over my sexual urges. I admittedly have a past strewn with casual relationships and often criticize myself for not controlling these urges. Should I not have learnt to deal with my sexual cravings and not succumb to temptation? Or am I not in fact only responding to a natural, healthy human desire? Is it irresponsible for two consenting adults to participate in safe sex? Was I taking advantage unknowingly of a vulnerable woman who was desperate for affection? I hate rhetorical questions. My conscience however, evaporated as hastily as it had appeared as a hand moved slowly up the inside of my thigh.

I had planned to spend only one night, but due to the circumstances that prevailed I easily persuaded myself that I deserved a day's rest. Elena emerged from the shower unselfconsciously displaying her naked body and began her meticulous cleaning routine. My hastily discarded clothes that lay in a heap on the couch, where I was supposed to have slept, were folded neatly and put away. I lay back in bed lazily admiring my accidental nude servant come landlady dance to the beat of Sean Paul as she prepared my breakfast. She claimed to enjoy cooking for others but disliked eating. Her large breasts swayed and she was unabashed' when one accidentally dislodged a piece of toast from her plate.

I was a little relieved when she eventually stormed out the door for work having first instructed me on the painstaking procedure for the multi-lock door. She was loud and abrasive and although I was enjoying her competitive sexual appetite, I knew who the boss in this relationship was. I was told to wait in the apartment like a diligent boy scout and prepare for the next round of my not unpleasant punishment.

After a long hot shower, I shaved and lay on the couch enjoying awful American day time TV. Strong coffee made my hands shake. I ventured out feeling like a naughty teenager skipping class. The street was a teeming vegetable market where wrinkly faced women did brisk business and gypsies sold cheap Chinese souvenirs. I bought a bowl of what looked like stew from a vendor for a brittle old lady who sat bent double on the pavement and received a cackle and a pat on the head for my troubles. Getting my hair cut was a comical event of miscommunications. I left thanking them profusely while thinking a blind armless kangaroo on cocaine would have done a vastly superior job.

The boss arrived back from work early and caught me in the act of devouring her ice cream supply while watching soft porn on her computer. Needless to say I was disciplined for my misdemeanours. Once satisfied, yet another obsessive cleaning session was instigated. I returned to my position on the couch, cradled the laptop and opened a file named, 'Things to do in 2008'. This had seemingly been given a huge amount of thought and already some were completed. 'Sleep with a woman,' and 'Learning salsa dancing,' were still to do; 'Improve Arabic,' and spend 'More time with Grandmother,' were apparently already achieved.

I have never understood why people strive to live their lives by a 'to do' list. I consider having specific goals to be important but planning one's every action in advance and not merely enjoying whatever may unfold seems ridiculous to me. To be so regimented is to deny the thrill of spontaneity, giving in to a life of 'should' as opposed to 'want.'

I couldn't help chuckling at some of Elena's private ambitions and although I knew I 'should' feel ashamed of my actions, I was in a strange, rebellious mood. She enjoyed serving but made it clear, with her demeaning remarks about my manliness, who had the control in our charade of a relationship. I sang along to corny Eric Clapton songs, knowing full well it was irritating as hell, but my voice petered out when I came to number 67 and 68 on the list in front of me. Seemingly low on her priorities were 'Marry a foreigner,' and 'Get pregnant.' The words yelled at me louder than the Hoover head which was being undesirably thrust into my crotch by a smirking roommate.

What ensued was an awkward evening of me playing hard to get, swearing that I had everything from jaundice to lice, eating unhealthy amounts of raw onion and garlic, farting and burping like a deflating skunk, peeing all over the toilet seat and floor for good measure, making callous racist remarks and just about every other pathetic thing I have ever previously done in order to dissuade a girl from wanting to sleep with me. Her determination was relentless and although I knew she was having doubts about this stranger she had invited into her home, she could not ignore her desire to succeed. We compromised with a quick series of awkward thrusts and lip denting kisses. I am not adverse to a bit of erotically inspired pain but her wild hair-pulling, slapping, neck-squeezing and blatant disregard for my health, left me with more cuts and bruises than the attempted robbery a few weeks before. My yelps were treated with more mockery of my masculinity. It was not playful as with Katya but seemed as if she had a vendetta to inflict as much pain as possible on me and was probably just.

It was an uncomfortable morning as Elena surprisingly pleaded with me not to leave. She sulked and refused to talk as I packed up my belongings. I thanked her for her hospitality before pedalling away fast into a quagmire. I became enveloped in mud as I negotiated small chocolate lakes and became temporarily blinded by trucks' spray but enjoyed the restart of my adventure. The valley was shrouded in thick mist reminding me of my time in New Zealand.

The road climbed, my legs straining under the tension of the pedals, until I reached fields covered in a blanket of old snow. I passed beautiful rolling white hillsides, haystacks with white caps and a lone old woman who stood rubbing her hands together in the doorway of a small isolated church. The bad road became worse until I rolled into the muddy courtyard of a small motel.

After a good sleep I emerged to a wonderful world of falling snowflakes fluttering effortlessly in the air and I almost crashed several times on the early morning icy road due to lack of concentration. I was invited by three fellas to venture into the forest in search of wood and although tempted, was put off by movies of sharpened hatchets, mouths of yellow teeth and crossed eyes.

The gorge towered over the road dispelling little waterfalls and metre long icicles. High above, trees decorated in a glittering frosty snow peaked out from a thick cloud cover. A train track magically clung to the cliff face, supported by concrete pillars and suddenly disappeared into the mountain. The river raged below.

The snow thinned until I emerged once again onto a monotonous windswept plain. My mind had wandered, thinking about diving in Costa Rica when suddenly a crazed canine darted from the undergrowth. I tried to outpace it but it refused to give up chase. I sensed trouble when an echo of barks emanated from the surrounding village, signifying that the troops were gathering. After the attacks over the previous weeks I had, only days before, attached a long sharp nail to the end of my extendable pump. I would not consider myself a cruel person but when I need to defend myself I do so without compromise.

I gripped my weapon in my right hand ready to smack my manic shadow as two more wet mongrels emerged several yards ahead. The smaller but more agitated of the two charged his scrawny body forward kamikaze style, hitting my front left bag and making the bike swerve. I wrestled to regain control and left the dog dazed. My legs pumped hard attempting escape, not wanting the irritation of having to find a doctor for a rabies shot. Now on the main street, I was amused to see a pack of over twenty dogs of all shapes, shades and sizes following me, yapping and growling themselves into a frenzy.

Groups of locals sat whiling away their endless boredom. I was at first angry at their lack of concern but realized they were as helpless to control these beasts as I was. I felt I had invented a bizarre new festival called, 'Cycling With The Dogs' and I was the main attraction. In order to entertain the spectators and for want of keeping my legs intact, I teased one mongrel up close, drew my arm back and swiftly

Curious Companions

brought the nail down just above its ear. Its squeal was music to my ears as it skidded to a halt in front of what I imagined to be a cheering group of admiring onlookers.

My determination increased as the injured dog's comrades were not in the least dissuaded by my cruelty and began to swarm all around. I swung madly and missed my targets repeatedly. This escapade had been going on for some minutes and I began to tire. Another approach was needed so without any ethical considerations, I lured one of my most vicious opponents to my left and veered slowly across the road. I could clearly see the dog's absolute concentration on my twirling legs, its salivating tongue hanging from its mouth. As we rounded a tight bend I swerved suddenly first into then away from the dog, leaving it confused. That was the moment it froze knowing it had been defeated as a lorry pummelled its body into the tarmac. It went thudding under the wheels without even a chance to whimper.

Of course my conscience was at play but more for my fellow road user than for this God-forsaken creature. Thankfully I received a friendly wave from the driver who was no doubt quite used to the experience of extinguishing canine nuisances. The many rotting corpses on the roadside, one frozen stiff on a bed of snow, another floating in a pool of mud, illustrated the insignificance of their lives. My adversaries had finally succumbed and stood looking at each other embarrassed on the blood stained road. I spent the day perfecting this technique and left a trail of mutilated dogs in my wake.

4

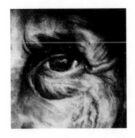

Sweet Sixteen

I roamed the rubbish strewn streets of Rovinari in search of food under the shadow of yet another gruesome power station. Packs of dogs terrorized pedestrians. A dozen horse carts galloped, returning home in the near dark. Their passengers waved happily and spurred me on. I pleaded for shelter at a hotel under renovation and the kind big bearded, big bellied owner agreed to give me a room if I didn't mind waiting an hour for the workmen to stop their drilling and the dust to settle.

I felt self-conscious as the barmaid and two friends talked, unconcerned about hiding their quizzical glances. Adrian the owner was sociable and astonished when I told him the distance I had come. He also told me about the difficult times during Communism when he could have been imprisoned for associating with a foreigner. He warned me about the evil people residing in neighbouring Bulgaria. 'Mafia have all this country,' and 'you good for kidnapping,' he shouted, agitated by my lack of concern.

Here I was in Romania, a country with a dire reputation for crime and I was being advised to arm myself against a supposed threat in a country he had never been to. I would have preferred to be 'good for kidnapping' than heed his hollow warnings.

As is typical amongst men with little in common, our conversation soon turned to women – a universal language of admiration and longing. Adrian was happily married but told me he liked to have fun with the waitress whom he labelled, 'free, unlucky, not pretty.' She was indeed quite repellent and Adrian snorted loudly as he recounted having to always close his eyes.

Mike owned the local car sales station. His claim to fame was that he once slept with a Ukrainian prostitute. We all laughed and pounded the table when he explained that as an immature twenty five year old he had proposed, having just lost his virginity to the woman twice his age. Her response was that he was not well enough endowed to satisfy her as a husband.

Bottle after bottle of beer appeared in my hand and somehow I found myself drunkenly swatting thin air in an attempt to play table tennis. The gathering had swelled over the hours and amongst the crowd a young girl sporting a pair of skin tight white shiny trousers and a red top that defined her curves, chatted to the barmaid. She looked fantastically inappropriate standing precariously in her high heels amongst the sawdust. She belonged in a dark nightclub with loud trance music and too many flashing lights, not a snack bar amongst poor farmers whose horses were tied up out front and who thought table tennis was a revelation in modern entertainment.

Mike had seen me smiling at the young blonde who in my inebriated state resembled a Swedish goddess. She was no older than seventeen. As I explained my story for the umpteenth time, with animated sign language, to a group of beefy men, Mike approached with Silvia. He playfully patted her on the ass and told her to sit. I was quite happy for her to join our table but almost swallowed my tongue when she plonked down on my lap. The room laughed and cheered. I grinned sheepishly, Silvia blushed. She was obviously nervous but reached an arm around my back.

'She like you for sex please!' Mike said eloquently as he tossed a packet of condoms onto the table.

My intoxicated bravado was over-inflated. I joked with the crowd as to why only one packet was available. Our sexual encounter seemed to be the highlight of everybody's night and people cheered again as another packet and several individual contraceptives of various colours were donated. I wondered if her parents were amongst the encouraging

Curious Companions

revellers. I offered my thanks and was grateful to deflect some attention as Adrian began snogging his staff member, eyes tightly closed. A skinny man began to sing a song, the crowd clapped and stamped their feet eagerly. Silvia refused her own chair when our friends got up to join the sing song and instead sat giggling as I held her leg. She knew no English and insisted on holding my beer for me to drink from.

As an argument brewed I saw my opportunity to escape, so grabbed the pile of condoms, ushered Silvia up the stairs, drunkenly slapping her on the ass, before falling to my hands and knees on the hall floor. I leaned on my stilettoed friend as she fumbled with the door key.

For the past hour I had debated whether I could yield to my lust for this beautiful young girl but yet again my conscience was a reminder of the realities of the situation. There was no doubt she wanted to spend the night with me but I expected, like Elena, she too may be unprepared for the disappointment when I inevitably deserted her in the morning.

She turned on the TV as I went to the bathroom in search of a sobering device. When I returned she was bopping around the uncarpeted floor in her underwear mesmerized by the music of Beyonce. I stood in the doorway relishing the sight before me and thinking how great it was to be young and single. She was extremely hyper now and threw her arms around my neck, like the excited teenager she was. I urged her onto the bed where we lay enveloped in each others arms, my mind in turmoil. She looked at me with big blue eyes, a combination of uncertainty and innocence. I tried to explain how much I wanted her but thought she might regret what she now thought inevitable. Her face was subtly illuminated in the dark room and I became silent, admiring her pale complexion, unblemished cheeks, button nose and perfect lips. I wished she could understand when I told her how beautiful she looked.

We kissed slowly, our lips loitering together. I fought the intensifying desire that was building inside me. Her nervousness was overflowing, her hands trembled and were hesitant. She copied me as I stroked the smooth skin of her face. I felt overwhelmed by her timidity.

To reject her would inevitably leave her confused and disappointed but I knew I could not continue. Better to hurt her feelings now than abuse her innocence.

Before I set off on this bicycle trip I had thought a lot about what might happen throughout the months but not once did I expect sex to figure. Admittedly being a male in my twenties, I am not unusual for placing sex quite high on my daily list of priorities, but lying there in a half built hotel room, somewhere in South East Romania with a stunning teenage girl who I could not communicate with was pretty unexpected.

She shivered as the cold night air made goose pimples of her skin. I grabbed some blankets and pulled her close to me. She looked puzzled but seemed to accept that we would not be getting any more physical than we had already been. She smiled as I kissed her on the nose, giggled when I pinched her bottom and let out a tentative squeal as I tickled under her arms. She innocently took my hand once again in hers.

The click of the door closing woke me from my drunken slumber. The bed was empty and a sense of abandonment hit me worse than I had worried it would the girl. It struck me as hard as the hangover that was making my head vibrate and my mouth taste as if I had taken to cleaning the floor with my tongue during the night. I located my water bottle and cursed my weakness to the lure of alcohol.

I left money on the bed for my night's stay and crept out the back, fearing interrogation about the previous night's endeavours. I had been accepted unquestionably by these unpretentious and benevolent people and although I knew they deserved at least a good bye, I cowered away under my jacket against an onslaught of torrential rain.

The muscles Break above my knees were unexpected casualties of the worst roads I'd encountered so far. Every bump sent painful shockwaves up my legs. Potholes hid slyly beneath dark pools of

Curious Companions

water and I doubted the surface had been repaired since the days of Communism. I could no longer ignore the pain as I recoiled with every downward push.

A café outside of Craiova was a dull affair. Teenagers resented my interruption of their game of cards. A group of men wearing impressive fur coats and matching hats sipped small glasses of wine and whispered. I removed my soggy shoes and thawed my feet on a lukewarm radiator. I wished Silvia were there to keep me company. I tried to overcome the angst of loss. Two inquisitive guys approached but I was too tired for politeness so remounted and continued into the bleak countryside. It was so cold that when I removed my gloves to adjust my bags it took fifteen agonizing minutes to regain any sensation.

I attempted to eat sardines on bread, sitting on a tree trunk surrounded by barren fields, nappies, egg shells and tin cans at my feet. I felt dejected and alone and threw my revolting lunch to the crows. I devoured my last kiwi and pondered on how a tropical fruit had ended up there on that desolate icy plain. Snowflakes filtered through the air. I stared at my muddy feet. A grave was adorned with plastic flowers meant to last a lifetime but already faded by the harsh climate. Columns of goats, herded by men cocooned in wild looking fur skins, snaked their way across frozen pastures. Dormant train tracks ran into the void and a red signal seemed hypnotic in its vibrancy. An abandoned concrete pylon kept watch over the jagged edge of an iceberg sprinkled with a layer of white powder. Horses poked half-heartedly at a mound of silage. I could sense they knew there was more to life.

Along the never ending streetscape, old men leaned on gates chatting to their neighbours and women, cloaked in shawls, leisurely turned well handles. Their children pursued hysterical chickens and feeble old grannies sat on benches gazing into the abyss, looking thoroughly stoned.

I arrived in Caracal with only my left leg propelling me. Every second building seemed derelict and rubble was discarded in mounds along the broken streets. The hotel in the main square had been closed down some years before. I gazed in the window of an 'Irish Bar' also

Curious Companions

abandoned. The town was a miserable place at best. I was greeted with looks of suicidal aspirations. I felt I had landed up in a town condemned and forgotten by the modern world.

After limping around the quagmire of back streets I found an old rusted bus concealing the entrance to what was the only hotel in town. The receptionist was not the least bit happy to see a customer arrive and did his utmost to dissuade me from staying in his 'unsuitable' establishment. My muddy raingear soiled the floor as he reminded me that the hotel only had two stars and would not be able to provide the creature comforts I was most probably accustomed to. I scratched my unshaven beard, picked mud out of my hair and faked horror at there not being a swimming pool or an en-suite Jacuzzi. He looked at me with a wry smile, angry thoughts prompted me to lock him in the cupboard. I thanked him profusely, gave him the night's rent and told him I'd prefer never to see his scrawny spiteful face again. Due to my lack of courtesy I was given what was probably the dead dwarf janitor's room for the night. The mattress dipped in the middle like a hammock. I lay flat, scraping mould from one wall with my toes as my head stroked flaking paint from the other.

Food was now a priority. I kicked a plastic bottle along the street with a flip-flop footed boy. I ate kebabs and too many Turkish sweets in a café where gypsy kids came in search of spare change and pity and received neither.

After shopping, I hobbled towards the hotel but realized I was being followed by another group of scruffy kids who had been loitering outside the supermarket. I made a few turns hoping they would lose interest but they kept a safe distance. It had been a long day and totally devoid of patience I turned around suddenly to confront them. There were five grubby faces, all aged from eight to fourteen. One confident boy wearing a ripped purple hoody stepped up and shouted indignantly at my stomach. He peered up to see the reaction on my face but when I motioned for him to 'feck off', the slippery bag of milk fell from my hand and plopped onto the mud. I felt ridiculous as I bowed at the youngster's feet to retrieve my breakfast. Seeing his opportunity, my miniature antagonist swiped at the jiggly bag with his Wellington boot, sending a white stain across the road. Before I could rise I received a swift kick in the back of the leg for added embarrassment. I groped in my shopping bag searching for something more appropriate than my fists to defend myself against these little ruffians. I brandished a twelve inch salami and thwacked the tallest one over the head. My opponents hooted with laughter. I am all for giving less well off children more joy in their lives but never before did I consider this approach. Two elderly men out for their evening stroll waved so I put down my floppy weapon. The kids had begun to chastise the teen that lay in the dirt clutching his reddened face so I crept away pleased with my evening of goodwill.

The dawn was a picturesque world of fresh snow. The flawless cover obscured the filth beneath. I followed creaking carts, turning my pedals with the rhythm of horse's footsteps. In Alexandria, I asked an inquisitive young guy the whereabouts of a hotel. Although he had no English he led me around the dreary city with eternal patience. He had a long stride, chain-smoked and looked behind to check out a passing girl's ass. Hotels were either closed or radiculously expensive. Standing on a street corner he stuttered about a hotel while gesticulating to himself. He came close to my face, talking slowly as if I was mentally retarded. Seeing nothing was registering he tried a different approach, shouting as if I was deaf.

We crept into his bedroom where his older brother Alex was asleep under a mound of blankets. He sat up surprised, adjusted his woolly hat and introduced himself in impeccable English. He talked with annoying yet impressive precision for someone who had never been beyond Romania's borders. He was a computer engineer and obviously highly educated. His education had no doubt been given priority over that of his younger brother, who was an unemployed PVC window installer.

I was installed in a pair of ancient cords and pink frilly sandals and introduced to their youthful mother. I assumed she was their sister and she blushed as innocently as a little girl in response to my compliments. They delighted in hosting such a rare foreign tourist yet I felt selfish for stuffing my face with their precious food. Their aunt fussed over me placing a fur coat over my shoulders to stem the cold. My four new friends sat on the couch smiling and observing my every

Curious Companions

move. The aunt was dispatched to buy some nasty soda drink which I diligently drank with exaggerated pleasure.

We went to a museum. It was closed. We visited a friend in his thirties who sat surrounded by a collection of electrical equipment. He chatted online to a fourteen year old girl from Portugal and proudly showed us photos of her in erotic poses. I had a strong urge to smack him in his creepy, paedophilic face. Of course my hypocritical side was raring its ugly head once again.

I felt disappointed by the criticism they aimed at 'all Romanian people', their 'incompetent attitudes' and 'lazy work ethics'. Alex apologized profusely for not having a nightclub in the town and would not listen when I explained that they are overrated in my opinion anyway. Johnny shouted at me as if I'd lost my hearing aid and creepo asked me to compose a birthday message to his 'girlfriend' half his age.

We sat in a depressing bar hall frequented by groups of similarly bored men. The beers were good and I drank with gusto. The guys wanted to know about my sexual history and even though I only admitted to sleeping with a few women they became overwrought with silent jealousy.

We scoffed *shoarmas* in the dimly lit street as Alex criticized Romanian election policies. A persistent gypsy pestered me about where I was staying and the guys became irritated, telling him in no uncertain terms where to go. A group of his unscrupulous friends waited nearby and I knew a fight was imminent. I put my arm around the thug's shoulder and led him aside. We spoke in Spanish as he had relatives living there and was probably better at the language than I was. I confessed to not having any *Leu* but asked if he liked American money. He puffed out his chest and said he would accept it. From my back pocket I took out a bunch of notes, counted out a couple of hundred and placed them in the youngster's dirty hand. I patted him on the back and told him I would see him in America.

As we strolled off Johnny was even more exasperated than usual having seen his honoured guest robbed of precious money. It took the majority of the walk home for the others to explain to him that monopoly money was not legal tender.

I was shown the backyard where I was instructed to crap wherever I would enjoy it. I anguished over not wanting to make a mess in the shed or the middle of the yard, so eventually chose a corner under the spotlight of a street lamp. It was a long night of tedious tiptoeing around in the cold and dark as I succumbed to a volcanic bout of diarrhoea. We slept three to a bed and dressed up in more clothes than we wore when outdoors.

5

Hostility, Herb and Harassment

The family watched me bathe as I knelt top naked over a basin. The giggling aunt poured warm water over my head and the mother rubbed shampoo into my scalp. I haven't been bathed by another person since the days when I shared the bath with my brother as a child and felt a tad embarrassed.

We congregated by their picket fence for an obligatory photo before I departed. The wind disrupted my progress. I became irritable and cursed staring donkeys. At a shady bar there was no food, no hot drinks, no electricity, no heat and no server. I helped myself to a coke, left some change on the counter and sat holding a feisty cat for the only source of warmth. Men with leather jackets stared blankly but responded with wheezy grunts to my greeting.

Through the metal grilled windows I could see a gathering of the local populace around my bike and suddenly realized I had not used my lock. Not only this but I had subconsciously stopped using it for over a week and didn't even know where my keys were. Ironically I was in the poorest country in Eastern Europe yet I had no fear of my possessions being stolen. My bike was worth approximately what these impoverished farmers earned in a year but I felt completely at ease in their presence.

A lock can be cut, broken or picked with little effort and I considered it to be more of a hindrance than a help. To pull up outside an establishment such as this and begin to securely lock my possessions away from the curious crowd would only imply distrust and therefore create an instant barrier. People would feel obliged to rob me as a matter of principle. To show my confidence in their honesty and greet people as equals has, in my experience, left no regrets. Maybe I am a naive idealist but to create unwarranted divisions due to negative preconceptions seems blatantly foolish.

A snowy plateau merged with the sky, obscuring the horizon. Only telephone poles disturbed the untouched white canvas. Cold air tore at my cheeks and tears filled my eyes. I discovered that I had taken a foolishly long route and what was supposed to be a relatively short day to the border became a thirteen hour ordeal. Insanity and retardation seemed to be endemic. One inbred male grunted out a loud 'uggggggh' with wildly swinging arms and looked at me with mouth open as if keen to hear an equally incoherent reply. Pain shot up my legs as I negotiated the unintentional, yet extremely effective, succession of speed bumps that plagued the road. I dodged idiots who ran in my path and screamed out for the God-forsaken day to end. I envied people who had never been there.

The bright lights of Bulgaria lit up overhead, welcoming me in the dark. I grinned pathetically at the border police, overjoyed with having overcome the torturous day. I had expected a quick glance at my passport and a congratulatory pat on the back as I'd received at the Romanian border but here I had my first encounter with power zealous border police.

'What is this?' The podgy officer demanded, having snatched my passport from me.

'It is my passport,' feeling ridiculous for stating the obvious.

'What is this?' He repeated. I began to think there had to surely be something in the water to make people so daft in this part of the world. Looking at the photo page, he groaned, 'What is this?' Adamant it wasn't me.

I asked politely what the problem was and with this he shut the book in irritation and pointed to my bike, 'What is this?'

I stared at the over-inflated oaf, unsure of how to answer without appearing to mock. I explained where I had come from and about my intended stay in his country but not even my compliments would budge the scowl from his face. He demanded evidence of travel insurance which I dismissed possibly a little too derisively. We stood on the tarmac, he – straight-backed with authority and jacket proudly displaying his status, me – rubbing my hands and doing a little dance to stem the numbing cold looking comical.

'No travel insurance, no entry.'

'But I don't need travel insurance.'

'Yes ok good no entry. You health insurance?'

'Nope sorry don't have that either.'

'Why not?'

'Because I don't need it.'

'Yes good no entry.' Smile. 'You Irish, why not passport British?'

'Ah because Ireland is now a Republic and no longer part of Britain,' I replied, raising my voice over the noise of a revving engine.

'Crazy stupid boy, Ireland is Britain.' He strutted off to a nearby cabin supposedly in order to see if I was on any of Europe's most wanted lists or to educate himself on Ireland's ninety years of independence.

Eventually, a little man emerged and stood on steps looking up at me. He talked as if he was on Speed, head twitching uncontrollably, eyes unable to settle. He spoke to me in Bulgarian, his voice moving from a loud shriek to a sombre whisper and back. Realizing he understood not one word of English and was sent out to aggravate me, I told him how he suffered from an acute inferiority complex, had probably never been laid and from the looks of his big belly would never be able to. Staring into my eyes he began to imitate me, 'Blah blah blah uhhhh,' his fat tongue dangling out.

It took unmerciful restraint to prevent myself from kneeing the imbecile in his bald head. Leaning forward, face contorted into a grimace, he waved my passport teasingly while yelling, 'Ahh mamamaa.'

I had had enough of these knob jockeys so grabbed my passport from his chubby little hand and told him to go fuck a donkey.

Pedalling away I ignored the indignant shouts from over my shoulder but paid attention when the barking began. A single Alsatian exploded from the cabin followed by the first official, grinning, overjoyed at my stupidity. The guard dog was a trained human hunter and sped across the pavement with the urgency of an animal not having been fed for some weeks. His powerful legs propelled him at an astonishing speed and I think both my legs and heart stopped in fear. Just as the creature was about to pounce I drew my pump with as much ferocity as I could muster down on its neck. A loud squeal came as the animal crashed into the bike leaving us tumbling onto the cold concrete.

I scrambled back onto my bike none the worse for wear and the dog hobbled into a dark bush. I had drawn blood and was not inclined to stick around for another interrogation at best. Images flashed in my mind of an international incident in the papers, 'Young Irish man goes insane. Murders innocent dog and attacks police on Bulgarian border.' A little shaken I joined the blinding traffic and snuck like an escaped convict to a nearby hotel.

The security guard cum receptionist was a colossal man of nearly seven feet and three hundred pounds. I felt apologetic as he squeezed into the tiny reception booth. His leather jacket was so big I thought I'd probably struggle to lift it. He fumbled with a set of keys and although unlocked, was unable to open the money drawer for lack of space. He was a gentle giant and told me I could pay in the morning.

The only other customers in the restaurant were two dodgy looking guys. They ordered the waitress around with grunts and waves of the hand. I had been warned about the notorious Bulgarian mafia. Kidnappings, shootings, corruption, brotherhoods and everything else that makes up a good movie were, I had been assured, part of everyday life there. One guy had a shaven head and although short was obviously the leader of the two. Their heads were bent low in deep conversation, their necks garlanded in gold chains. They smoked non-stop, their fingers also covered in bling. The lanky chap scratched his scalp in earnest and bobbed his head vigorously agreeing with his mentor. I speculated about what plot they were conjuring up or what heist they were reminiscing about. I yearned to be involved.

When I paid my bill the waitress presumptuously kept the change. Although only a few Euro, I was annoyed at her ignoring my beckoning call. I walked up to the counter and ordered an additional ice cream and pancakes and when it arrived carried it up to my room, instructing her to take for it out of the change. I felt pleased with my ingenuity although conscious of my extreme pettiness.

The next morning I spent an enjoyable hour shopping at an enormous supermarket, marvelling at the vast variety of products, having spent the past week eating whatever limited supply of food was available. At the check-out I proudly piled up my chocolate mousses, pastries and fresh fruit, only to be stumped when asked for my Metro Card. It turned out after a lot of confusion that this was in fact a members only supermarket and I was handed an application form in Cyrillic script.

A kind young woman offered to help me with my application to acquire food but warned it would take two weeks for approval. I laughed at the thought of a card portraying the proud owner to be an authorized and respected food buyer. Being accepted into the prestigious BMFPC (Bulgarian Metro Food Purchasers Club) would make my parents so very proud. I tried to bribe the cashier into selling me the goods I had so painstakingly chosen but alas, left empty handed.

I had found a flat tyre that morning and had pumped it to see if there was a slow puncture. I fought to hold my footing, slipping and sliding on the ice, trying to once again examine the deflated wheel. Not surprisingly I found a sharp piece of metal protruding through the tyre, a result of being cussed the previous evening and a warning that even pretty smiling waitresses should not be messed with in this country.

Two kilometres down the road an open backed truck revved up close behind me, blowing its horn in disgust at my presence. The vehicle sped past so close that its mirror smacked me on the shoulder, propelling me up over the footpath and luckily into a cluster of bushes. I scrambled to my feet cursing but feeling incredibly lucky not to have rebounded into the line of oncoming traffic. If even a few inches closer or a little faster, I would have surely lost control and nose dived into the pavement. It was a stark reminder of how careful I needed to be, although I knew I only had limited control over my safety.

The undulating countryside of stark snowfields reminded me of Christmas time visiting my grandparents in the south west of England. The views across the deep valley distracted me from the bustling streets of Veliko Tarnovo. The rooftops were white with snow and the river sparkled in the sun far below.

I met up with Milena on the steps of the football stadium and walked the short distance to her flat, shared with five fellow students. She was a bubbly girl and urged me to fill up on delicious homemade food posted to her by her parents. She liked the sound of her own voice but conversation was fractured as I was now tired and sore after a gruelling day.

She practiced her German and recited lines from an erotic book she was studying. Her excitable flatmates arrived and we began to devour the five litres of homemade wine. The table was full of snacks, liquors and wine and after an hour the twelve of us were making quite a racket. They were intrigued by my trip and swore to seek revenge from the border police. I felt privileged to have this party organized for my visit even though being the centre of attention was draining.

Well inebriated, joints were rolled. Not normally partaking in such vices I deliberated before declaring why not. Although being able to handle my liquor, smoke does strange things to my mind. Before long, I sat speechless. My mouth dried and as wine was the only drink available, I drank myself into a stupor.

I felt incredibly self-conscious as I struggled to join the conversation, not knowing what to say and anyway having lost the ability to talk. People looked at their guest with confusion and eventually returned to their own language. Unsure of what was being said I was overcome with paranoia. People's inflated laughs were surely directed at me. I pulled embarrassed smiles, nodded enthusiastically and drank shots thrust into my hand.

I fretted over what to do and tried desperately to talk to my neighbour but as luck would have it he had little English. He looked at me with as much disdain as a passerby asked by a drug addict to withdraw a needle from his venous arm. The overweight black cat stared at me with intense yellow eyes and I began to believe it was

Curious Companions

telepathic. Paranoia made me sweat. I dried my forehead with my t-shirt and thought about jumping out the window.

It was now well into the night and the munchies took a firm grip. My perspective was confused, my focus blurred. I fumbled over a plate of salami and chewed greedily like a squirrel with both hands. They were a great group of genuine, open-minded, generous and enthusiastic youngsters, yet I felt like a Communist English black man living in Sneem in 1942. Out of place. A pariah.

There was no doubt I had been a drunken and stoned fool that night but at breakfast we all had a good laugh at the photos taken. I winced in shame. I cursed my throbbing head wishing I had absconded before the heavy drinking had begun.

The air was fresh, the pavements icy. My eyes were misty as I moped around the streets. The climb to the Patriarch Church was well worth the effort as the murals were spectacular. I sat alone in the ruined fortress for hours enjoying the views and the solitude. I munched cake in a lively café as a procession of stylish women paraded by. Their boyfriends had impeccably polished shoes and I dreaded the day I ever get trapped by a woman of such high maintenance.

Milena and her friends considered the Romanian standard of living to be vastly superior to their own. I wondered what had fostered this feeling of being downtrodden and inferior when in fact every modern luxury and form of entertainment was available. Most had spent time in the UK or America and with the exception of earning less money, none had any regrets about returning home. They were annoyed however, at the huge influx of foreigners moving to their town, driving the property prices way out of reach of the average local. It was obviously big business as every second shop on the main street dealt in real-estate in English.

Later that evening with the girls dressed in the shortest of short skirts we piled into taxis to take us to a tequila bar. There we met a Nationalist from Catalunia and a Pacifist from Wexford. The former thought all Neo Nazis should be hung and had sympathies for terrorist organizations. The latter with the exception of killing Hitler and Stalin disagreed with all types of violence. The previous night's awkwardness had evaporated and we partied like old friends until the early morning.

Still well lubricated I packed up, clambered over last night's triumphant collection of shopping trolleys, cones and other public memorabilia and set off towards Bacho Kiro Caves in the purple haze of predawn. The canyon was steep sided and I followed a single set of footprints along the snowy path. A bored youth clad in army fatigues lounged on his bed in a little hut. I paid my minimal admission fee and entered the eerily quiet cave with only the pitter patter of water droplets to keep me company. The end of the slippery passageway opened into the Concert Hall Room, a twenty metre wide cave with perfect acoustics. My tin whistle filled the cave with Irish disharmony and I shivered alone reminiscing about home.

Next on the agenda was the highest climb so far. The road weaved through thick forest with snow piled high over my head lining the way. It had been compacted firm on the road and mixed with grit to clog up my brakes and mudguards and cause problems with my gears.

One of the most magical sights I have ever had the pleasure to witness was slowly unfolding. Snow had fallen on the bare tree branches and as this side of the mountain was perpetually in shade, had frozen stiff resembling cotton wool. Branches drooped with the weight and I felt I was engulfed in a fairytale. The forest's deep cover of snow was untouched and I pushed the bike along spellbound by the mystical beauty.

Although I did not want this enchanting world to end, I was relieved to find a motel sunk into the snow near the summit. I enjoyed every crunching step as I followed my sombre host across a deep field of white powder. The little wooden hut sat lonely amongst trees reminding me of similar lodgings by the beaches of Thailand. That day however, it was minus God knows how many degrees and I spent the evening lying on my bed spooning the radiator.

It had snowed so heavily during the night that my deep footprints had vanished. The first hour of the day was spent de-icing my steed and regaining blood circulation in all of my limbs. The view from the peak revealed a mountainside of white trees disappearing into silent mist. Branches resembled ice sculptures, crystals glittering in the day's first rays of sunlight.

Curious Companions

Having descended to the plains once more poverty reared its ugly head as dark skinned gypsies rummaged around landfill sights. Rubbish was strewn across a vast open countryside and people shouted at me with aggressive taunts. A group of six loitering teenagers in dirty rags stepped in my path but were unable to knock me from the bike. It was the most hostile area I'd crossed and I was surprised at the contrasts between the luxuries of Veliko Tarnovo and the slums I now found myself in.

That night I visited a restaurant down a back alley of a miserable town. It was a curious place with only a bad tempered man, his wife who sported a black eye and their less than adorable child as customers. The waitress was asleep with her head propped on a table, a piercing below her lip. She frowned, pointed at the kettle in response to my

Hostility, Herb and Harassment

request for tea and scoffed when I suggested something edible. I was startled to see a near life-size calendar of a woman reclining on a stool wearing only a pair of red and white striped socks, legs wide open for all to admire. The kid kicked the cat and threw an empty mug at me to the delight of his parents. Even the sugar packets were pornographic, depicting an assortment of naked women complete with obscene quotations. I drank fast, kicked the cat and went to bed with a streaming cold.

While living in Spain some years ago I had had some unpleasant experiences with Turkish immigrants and I was now battling to rid myself of the resulting feelings of prejudice before entering the country which connects Europe and Asia. These thoughts combined with the constant bombardment of negative images and news stories we receive via the media from the Islamic world, prevented me from feeling totally at ease.

The morning brought a fresh bout of optimism and my first singing minarets, as I cruised through customs and into Turkey. My belly was rebelling from lack of food so I stopped to eat in the courtyard of a petrol station. I was beckoned inside by two attendants. Tunay, a tall gaunt man with inch thick glasses had a little English which he forced out with the facial expression of someone with constipation. His overweight friend was not fond of words and sat staring at his grubby bare toes. We sipped scorching hot tea by a battered coal heater and chatted about our dissimilar lives. Their friend Sofia was twenty four and looked older than my mother. We ate a meal before I apologized for my haste and struck out into the wind once more.

Strong gusts caught hold of my bike and refused to let me achieve over five kilometres an hour. The packs of dogs that plagued me in Romania were back with a vengeance and I delighted in unadulterated satisfaction as I caught one after another of these snarling, repugnant beasts squarely on the head with baseball sized rocks. The petrol signs displayed an emblem of a dog's head as in

Romania, the only difference being instead of portraying a line of jagged teeth my tormenters now spouted fire from their nostrils. Tackling dogs equipped with internal flame throwers was not the kind of experience I had anticipated when dreaming of my journey through the Ottoman Empire.

That night I was forced to stay at a motel where the obnoxious owner and his friends treated me as if they had recently scraped me from their shoe. The owner glared at me from across the room, his face enveloped in cigarette smoke, his eyes a piercing hatred. I walked my bike through the hall and into my room ignoring shouts of indignation and glad to find a secure lock. I felt like a chicken cooped up in a dog pen but on my way out to search for food, I wished them a cheery good evening in the hope of diminishing the tension.

Next door I was surprised to find a huge restaurant with modern exterior and blinking neon lights. The interior was a pretentious mess of modern accessories but little substance. A huge room of circular tables surrounded a small stage. It was Saturday night and the only table occupied was a group of startled waiters playing cards.

I enquired if a table for one was available and was guided to an enormous table in the corner by the stage. Afraid they would have the arduous task of resetting, mine was the only one without a table cloth, flowers, napkins, cutlery or any of the flash items adorning every other of the hundred tables. My waiter rejoined the group so I sat writing until the courteous security guard invited me to eat food. He apologized for not having a menu as there was apparently only one set meal and I eagerly agreed as the curtains were beginning to look remarkably appetizing.

Large multi-coloured lights were turned on and mirror balls began to rotate. A fork was placed by my side and a pepper shaker was positioned carefully in the centre of the vast table. A waiter stood by my shoulder munching an apple while surveying my curious habit of writing. A bland soup was brought and I was urged to drink direct from the bowl. Another member of staff then sat across from me to blow smoke in my face.

A man wearing a penguin tuxedo appeared and I cringed as he checked himself repeatedly in his pocket mirror. His hair was glued to his scalp and he thoughtfully informed me that he was very beautiful. Seeing I had a camera he insisted on posing for photographs as my salad of lettuce and vinegar arrived. Not wanting to offend I obliged the pathetic man. His vanity was utterly revolting and I would have surely pummelled his pretty face with the pepper shaker had it not been so far away. He pulled supposedly sexy faces, sucked the tip of his finger, flexed his biceps and made me want to throw my camera at the group of admiring waiters.

The next course of grisly kebab was accompanied by a deafening wail of a ballad as Romeo pranced around the stage making my food even less inviting. I recoiled in my chair and ignored the singer who shrieked for my pleasure. I regretted having been born with eardrums and went to bed feeling mentally abused.

6

Winter Wilderness
and the Wonders of War

It was another difficult day, the blizzard thickened, snow cover became deep and I struggled to see even a few metres ahead. Keeping forward momentum was almost impossible as the tormenting wind blasted my side with such ferocity that I was sent sprawling several times. My pockets and sleeves filled with snow and I wrapped a t-shirt around my face to prevent frostbite. Blinded by the intense glow I donned my sunglasses. Snow piled up in long dunes horizontally across the road and I enjoyed bashing through these hillocks of light powder.

I was relishing this new challenge but wondered how far I could go before I would have to find shelter. The road was closed and abandoned cars were quickly becoming submerged. Tall apartment blocks appeared faint through the haze and lampposts whistled musically in the wind. Again I hurtled head first along the soft blanketed road and lay feeling strangely happy propped up against the central divider. Snowflakes swirled around me. A snowmobile came hurtling unexpectedly out of the white blur, oblivious to my presence. Ice congregated on my face mask and I began to worry about my numb hands. I was weak with hunger and grappled to open a stubborn packet of biscuits.

Out of the obscurity came two men, their heads cocooned in woollen scarves, their eyes hidden behind ski masks. They stood over

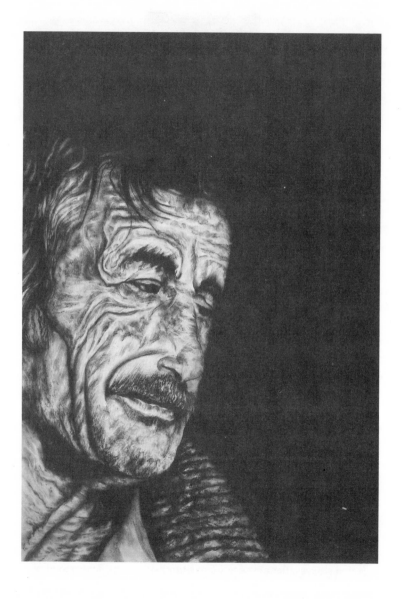

me bemused. We yelled at each for several minutes unable to hear over the howl of the wind. Exasperated, they ignored codes of conduct as one grabbed me by the jacket while the other dragged my heavy bicycle off the road.

Only some twenty metres away but invisible in the storm was a café. We burst through the doors followed by a flurry of snow, shattering the congenial atmosphere. Several dozen quizzical eyes met mine. I wished everybody a cheerful good evening and discarded a large pile of clothes and melting snow onto the concrete floor. I sat feeling privileged next to the central wood heater as steam engulfed my drying body. Pieces of homemade lunches were donated to me as I fumbled with my notebook trying to convert my gratitude.

Little work could be done on days like this so the male population gathered to play cards, read newspapers and gossip. The owner of the café was a kind man who force-fed me tea, his son was an intolerable pain. I felt like a museum exhibit as men took turns to stand by me and observe. They resembled ruthless outlaws. I took their intrigue as being complimentary.

My saviours were young truck drivers who had become stranded and on seeing me had feared a little more for my safety than my lack of sanity. Hussain translated my story to the congregation. He was a handsome twenty four year old and was awaiting the collection of a load of hay to be transported to Istanbul. Antilla was quiet, yet made it his duty to ensure that I was well looked after. Errol was built like a weightlifter on steroids, had bright blonde hair and went by the nickname of 'The Russian'. Mustafa was conservative, dressed in a tweed jacket and was the provider of the frozen hay. They were a congenial bunch and we spent the afternoon absorbed in cards.

Later on we were blown down a narrow street knee deep in powder, whooped, kicked snow in the air and slid along sheets of ice like kids on roller shoes. We passed a man bent double against the wind and were greeted by Mustafa's wife, Busra, and their two year old daughter, Asra. We lounged around on sofas before crossing our legs to eat course after course of delicious food on the floor. Much effort was put into the day's main meal and Busra seemed pleased when us men lay back holding our bulging stomachs. Her face was framed by a colourful scarf and her long flowery dress swayed as she frequently topped up our minute glasses of tea.

Although their English was minimal we discuss religion at length. I was eager to see what the average Turkish man thought of unreligious Western Europeans. They too were keen to understand my way of life. I explained how even though I was born into a Christian family I do not have strong religious beliefs. I clarified that I had the utmost respect for anyone who, by following a particular faith, lived a well meaning life of benevolence just as they were demonstrating to me. Mustafa fingered his prayer beads non-stop and I wondered what he was saying to his God. They told me that they admired my honesty and thought it was great that I was both free in body and in mind. We agreed religion caused too many misunderstandings, divisions and hatred in the world.

I had learnt that Islam is a system of rules for all aspects of life. This may seem to some like imposed restrictions as compared to the West's policy of democratic freedom, however, being the direct word of God they are, on the contrary, wholeheartedly welcomed and not resented as some might assume. I was finding it difficult to relate this to my own upbringing of independent thought. By questioning the world and my own actions I had developed ethics and morals. This clashed with these people's rigid belief that the words of the Koran were fact and thus questioning their correctness was profane. If I need guidance I seek within myself to formulate an answer from experience and knowledge, whereas my kind-hearted hosts turn without exception to the word of God. A variety of my questions were answered simply, 'Because our Lord Allah, Peace be upon Him, says it is so.' They had no desire for a practical explanation of why pork meat was forbidden to them nor did they care to know why they prayed five times a day.

Mustafa's brother arrived and bragged of bedding a Moldovan girl and even had a photo of her amongst a small pile of family and friends. I disliked him for staining our conversation. He ordered Busra around like a servant and claimed to indulge in heavy drinking whenever possible. He had no qualms with prostitutes as they were 'not religious women' and therefore apparently did not deserve respect.

He wanted to go to England and our mutual dislike grew as I dismissed his dream as improbable.

Mustafa handed around his bundle of creased photos which showed him in army fatigues while training near the Iranian border – military service in Turkey being compulsory. He pointed a machine-gun towards Iran as if to show his bravery. I questioned his distrust of what I had assumed would be a brotherly Islamic country but he was adamant they were as untrustworthy as every other country in the world. A pair of dark sunglasses perched on his nose and a cigarette dangled from his mouth. We teased him, saying it was in fact Sylvester Stallone and not Mustafa.

The conversation turned to my route through Turkey and according to them the trouble I would unquestionably encounter in the east. I told them I didn't expected any from Kurdish people which they vehemently objected to. They were convinced that I would be shot, for evidently Kurds have a 'thirst for blood' and are eager to draw attention to their 'evil' claim for an independent state. It was sad hearing these inhumane and contradictory statements from guys who had only minutes before been pacifists.

To stem the progressively distressing conversation I suggested a walk to the café in order to collect some things from my bike. They readily agreed so, after donning our numerous layers, we set off into the dark street. Pure white was illuminated by intermittent flickering street lights. Snow flakes fluttered down in silence as I gazed up into the darkness.

The guys were attracted to a game of cards like a pervert to a nudist beach so I resumed my position as umpire. Feeling like a circus monkey I was glad to have at least one trick I could perform. I sat in the centre of the crowded room playing my tin whistle with nervously shaking fingers. At first everyone stared blankly and continued to count their prayer beads. To my relief however, some of the old fellas began to clap timidly and before long everyone was boisterously jumping about in excitement. Even though the commotion drowned out the music, these men relished the spectacle. A chubby chap crashed from a rickety table where he had attempted a rendition of an accelerated belly dance to the tempo of an Irish jig. I felt utterly idiotic for having harboured reservations about these people and their religion and after some ferocious back-slapping left knowing that the only thing that could come between us was my own foolish misapprehensions.

The roads were firmly compacted with snow and the grooves from vehicles made progress slow. One lorry had capsized discarding metal pipes across the road, lines of trapped cars and trucks queued, their patiently waiting drivers cheered and clapped at my unsteady advance. Families shovelling snow from sunken driveways stopped to wave. A break saw me perched on the balcony of an abandoned house gazing out for the first time along a snow covered beach.

The treacherous five-lane motorway entering Istanbul resembled a long muddy cow pen and drivers used their horns to distract themselves from boredom. I was not particularly bothered by the ignorant motorists yet could not refrain from giving several the finger in search of entertainment myself.

I trudged the slushy streets later that night and sat alone watching sea gulls circle the phenomenal Blue Mosque's glowing spires. The thunderous call to prayer signalled time for bed.

For two days I ventured around the city, exploring spice bazaars, going on boat trips, visiting museums and palaces, yet found myself removed from the experience. I was exploring where I thought I 'should', yet with no real interest. What purpose did I have shopping for carpets or spices or queuing for hours to view shawls worn by some long dead overweight Sultan? I felt sadly predictable.

I have always had reservation about visiting houses of worship, whether a church, temple, synagogue or mosque. I dislike the fact that some are taken over as tourist attractions. I feel the act of prayer and being close to God is private and personal and should not be compromised because of the curiosity of others. Great if people can admire without intrusion but I have found this is often not possible.

Curious Companions

Despite my reservations, I admittedly enjoyed a short visit to the Sultanahmet Camaii (Blue Mosque) at sunrise. Shards of light pierced the stained glass windows and I lay on the plush carpet staring up at the intricately decorated dome while an old man vacuumed around me.

I battled with the Pakistani embassy for a visa, avoided a clingy grey haired Australian man in the spectacular Aya Sofia, ate kebabs with fishermen who lined the bridges and cringed at tour groups who obediently followed their loud mouthed, umbrella waving leaders. Men scraped ice from the street as elderly people fell down, unable to get up again. I ate hash brownies, craved ice cream at three a.m. and fell asleep cradling a delicate Japanese girl who cradled her guide book.

Leaving the city was quite pleasurable as I followed the river through an up-market area. Ladies in high heels walked their dogs, couples posed at expensive cafés and yachts bobbed about forgotten on the dock. The contrast between that world and the poverty and crime ridden areas only a few streets away was startling. The city was indeed a magnificent culmination of Western lifestyles and Asian culture and I knew I had failed to do it justice. Sea gulls squawked, the sun shone down brightly and I crossed a bridge into Asia.

A buck toothed policeman reprimanded me for using the dual carriageway and I meekly obeyed, spending the remainder of the day lost amongst backstreets. Several times I wasn't concentrating as I sped down hills trying desperately to find my way, only to clatter into potholes, buckling my rear wheel.

The top story in the news was that Turkey had sent ten thousand troops into Iraq to attack the Kurdish strongholds there. I selfishly hoped it wouldn't affect my trip although I knew thousands of lives would be irreversibly changed. The news reporter seemed hysterical as men clad in white ski jackets jumped from trucks and trotted off over a snowy incline to do their country proud. Some grasped their guns and shot across a wide open valley. Missiles were fired. Brave soldiers smiled.

I made my way slowly through dark intimidating forests. A handful of dormant villages dotted the undulating hillsides, the mosque's minarets the only source of colour in a bleak landscape. Little girls in pink head scarves chased me and I felt horrible seeing their faces of joy replaced by disappointment. I left the road to relieve myself but sank up to my waist in snow. Convoys of lorries passed in the opposite direction, their drivers looking sick with boredom. I jumped around waving a spoon and spilling cornflakes and in return received grins of broken rotten teeth and blasts of the horn.

A line of horrible new tower blocks covering a hillside was mirrored by a monstrosity of sprawling glass and concrete on another. Kizicahannan is known to be a spa resort town where people come to indulge in the luxuries of natural warm water. I was forced to stay at an ostentatious establishment which boasted of every possible treatment any sane person would go to great lengths to avoid. I locked myself in my room and spent the evening flicking channels between what seemed to be an equal amount of Islamic preachers and gyrating porn-stars. The big bearded man pointed his finger warning of Western sacrilegious pleasures, the girl spread her legs urging the viewer to call the number on screen. The cleric angrily slapped the table in condemnation, the girl writhed in make-believe pleasure.

My host in Ankara was Ozgur, a polite, well educated divorcee who swore that the secret to preserving one's youth was to stay single. We had a lot in common although his fascination with Samurai swords was a little intimidating. He was one of Turkey's well off minority and decorated his apartment with the latest electronic equipment and superfluous gadgets.

We discussed many world issues and I was again disappointed to hear him denounce all Kurdish people as criminal. I had read up on the situation of these persecuted people wanting to know what the

Curious Companions

population in the east of Turkey had endured since the PKK (Kurdish Workers Party) began their armed struggle in the late seventies.

Problems arose with the creation of the Islamic State. Turkey's Constitution declared a single nationality designation for all Turks, thus not recognizing ethnic groups. The Kurds' subsequent fight for an independent state encompassing all predominantly Kurdish areas within Turkey, Iran, Iraq and Syria began. More recently they have compromised in search of recognition and equal rights within Turkey. Their struggle has seen thousands of lives destroyed and an entire region overwhelmed by poverty.

The government's main strategy for assimilating the Kurds has been language suppression. Anyone who publicly or politically asserted their Kurdish identity or was found speaking or writing their mother tongue risked public harassment or prosecution. Although this bill has been revoked since 1991 and political efforts for a peaceful resolution continue, the problems seem to have escalated.

The innocent Kurdish population was my concern. I cared little for the alleged reasons for indiscriminate murder by the PKK or why the government was sending thousands of naive recruits to fight their own countrymen in another land. Innocent people were caught in the crossfire – murdered for sympathizing with the PKK, executed for complying with the government.

Guerrillas came from camps across the border in Iraq, intimidating local Kurdish families, attacking Turkish military and police outposts and slaying civilian community leaders. Targeted in particular were the government's paid militia, known as village guards, and schoolteachers accused of promoting forced assimilation. The PKK are renowned for indiscriminate acts of violence with no hesitation in killing fellow Kurds whom they considered collaborators. This in turn enabled the government to portray them as a terrorist organization and justify its own policies. These included the burning of eight hundred and fifty border villages to prevent the harbouring of insurgents and the forced evacuation of their populations to Western Turkey. Its tactics have resulted in hundreds of civilian casualties and turned thousands of innocent Kurds into refugees.

Ozgur showed me a newspaper article where in an interview in 2003 Recep Tayyip Erdogan, the Minister of Defence, stated, 'The Turkish government is gradually loosing patience as America continues avoiding taking military actions against the Kurd rebels in Turkey who are presently based in Northern Iraq.' This patience seemed to have come to an end after five years as we watched the invasion of Iraqi territory. Today instead of pictures of young heroic recruits jumping from lorries, there was the stark realization that war brings inevitable death. Mothers and fathers cried out in anguish, hands waving wildly exclaiming the horrors that had been suddenly inflicted upon them. They held photos of their sons just like those Mustafa had shown me. They pleaded with the camera for mercy and realizing it was helpless, collapsed in each other's arms.

The old city bazaar was a hive of activity as men with white prayer caps jostled with workers pushing heavily laden carts. Stall sellers announced shoes, copper ware and jewellery and a cluster of knife shops did surprisingly brisk business. Beggars with contorted legs sat patiently awaiting salvation and men ran about offering tea from glasses delicately balanced on a silver tray. I ate a delicious meal and watched eager little boys in miniature uniforms run in and out delivering lunches. Women glanced at their reflection in the window pane, not for vanity's sake, but to be assured of their concealment within their head scarves. A gang of boys of about eight fought furiously in the street, slapping and kicking each other to the muddy ground, adults walked by with indifference.

Two kids followed me up the steeply sloping streets to the ruined castle walls where we ate chocolate and gazed across a sea of shacks. Mothers holding their babies wrapped in blankets chatted on street corners, house walls were cracked and leaned at unconventional angles.

Back in Ozgur's neighbourhood, we relaxed at a chic café as women strolled about confidently wearing tight jeans, revealing toned figures. They drove soft-top sports cars, their faces thick with makeup and shades poised atop their perfectly groomed hair. What a day of contrasts it had been.

I joined irate Turkish men trying to negotiate the Pakistani visa process conducted in English. Though I sympathized with them I left

Curious Companions

triumphant with my thirty-day visa. To celebrate we drank Guinness all night with the future film makers of Turkish television, who made me feel embarrassed with their desperate need to seem 'Westernized' in my presence. However, the out-of-date warm cans of bitter beer were fantastic.

The roadside was an endless row of factories and I waved to groups of workers who scurried to and from lines of dilapidated buses. It reminded me of my time working in factories in Kerry, Limerick and Galway, when I had been constrained to a monotonous life dominated by work in order to merely survive. They looked out at me, solemn and miserable, having succumbed out of necessity, to the life of a robot. I hoped that they too would one day experience the feeling of freedom and adventure.

For a change, I enjoyed a tail wind which propelled me along at a dangerously high speed, overtaking cars and dodging branches that littered the road. Unsecured garden furniture was sent charging across lawns and flags ripped frantically at their poles.

That night I was invited to stay and eat at a school where I had enquired about accommodation but after scoffing my meal I was promptly escorted to a bus stand to catch a lift to the next town. The crowd was adamant that wolves would attack me and I was bundled into a mini-bus alongside a fearful old couple.

A kilometre down the road I placed my hand on the driver's shoulder and signalled that I had reached my destination. He looked at me in disbelief as I paid the fare for the thirty five kilometre journey and dragged my gear out onto the snow. He seemed worried, yet I think a little relieved having now realized how insane I was. I sat feeling destitute in the dark night.

It was several hours before I staggered across a white marble reception floor and leaned exhausted on the mahogany desk of a hotel. Japanese clientele, in perfectly pressed white clothes, watched me warily. A pool of water gathered around my feet as if I had wet myself.

I groaned and dropped my head on the counter as the scared looking receptionist swallowed hard and told me they were full.

Back outside I stared hypnotised at my faithful steed and for the first time felt ill at the thought of mounting again. I walked on feeling faint and shivering in the frozen night air until the lights of a petrol station appeared out of the mist. I stood gawking at shelves of motor oil and a smirking employee. I sullenly bought stale biscuits and putrid warm tomato juice and sat in the yard before the attendant led me with a comforting arm into the office. I offered him and his workmate biscuits and they returned looks of offence. They obviously felt slighted by my lack of entertainment value as I struggled to stay awake, unconcerned by their boredom. It was uncomfortable feeling that their generosity was more out of a sense of religious obligation than genuine kindness.

The pint-sized chap probed his nose with a chubby finger, chewed enthusiastically on a piece of newspaper and took a swipe at a mangy dog with his muddy boot. The other who had two wives, slapped the TV searching in vain for a decent reception and ogled an actress, no doubt seeking a third. I curled up on the floor unable to overcome my heavy eyes and fragile patience.

The furnace was on full blast and I was naturally given the dreaded position closest this evil contraption. My back felt as if it was alight, my face was taut from the heat and I leaked sweat. My sleeping bag was to my side but on seeing me in discomfort the tall guy with protruding teeth urged me inside, insisting on zipping me up. I pretended to be asleep and slowly pulled the bag from my dripping body in order to give myself at least a slight chance of survival but again he tucked me in like a baby. I didn't know whether to laugh or cry as I buried my head in my jumper. I fought my way out of my evil cocoon and fell out the door ignoring my protesting roommates. I lay on the freezing concrete feeling such incredible relief before I was physically dragged back into the cauldron of torture. I felt an intense desire to maim my saviours.

7

Nature's Magic
and the Struggles of Man

The barren countryside stretched out before me, bringing back memories of the Burren. The sky was a bruised purple with threatening dark rain clouds brooding low over hills. Fields of snow crust glistened and small flocks of birds darted about, the first animal wildlife I'd see in weeks. The world was silent except for the squeak of my pedals.

I was crossing the frozen plateau of central Turkey towards Cappadocia, a place I had longed to visit for many years. Three volcanoes located on the edges of the area had once deposited huge amounts of volcanic ash, lava and basalt, laying the foundations for today's curious landscape. This in turn was relentlessly carved by nature and the people who had lived there.

My feet and hands were numb and strong winds struck the side of my face. I had been eager to reach the guesthouse but as I freewheeled down the valley towards Goreme, I was so overwhelmed by the natural beauty that all my petty complaints vanished. Waves of hillsides in soft pinks and earthy ocres extended in every direction.

Dawn, the kind Scottish lady at the guesthouse, was pleasantly eccentric. She told me the story of how she had come to spend the past twenty five years in this idyllic hideaway. She wore a long colourful hand-woven skirt and cursed the falling snow. Her first child had been born in a nearby cave and the lines at the corners of her eyes and mouth did not mar her beauty. We joked over ice-cold beers before her energetic six year old bounded in wearing a Spiderman mask and reclaimed her attention.

That night I walked around the picturesque village, enjoying the soft glow of the street lights revealing irregular shaped buildings and towering rocks. Distracted, I lost my balance on a thick layer of ice and careered down a steep cobbled street, coming to an abrupt halt at the feet of an impassive elderly man. He greeted me with a blasé 'Salaam Aleykum' (Peace be unto you), as I desperately searched for my camera and my dignity.

Ortahisar was my first stop early the next morning where I climbed the slippery steps through rooms and passages carved out of the natural rock castle some four thousand years before. I sat in silence, breathing in the crisp morning air and felt utterly content. Canyons spiralled out from the town, their sides marked with windows peering sheepishly out of the shadows. Modern stone houses mingled with ancient caves dug from the rock far below and a mirage of pinnacles peaked out of the snow covered plateau as if escaping from the depths of the earth.

I moved onto the cave settlement of Zelve which had been an important Christian community and a major religious centre. The interior of the cave city was designed as a labyrinth of tunnels and shafts to confuse the enemy. Where the huge white cliff faces touch the ground, doors allow entry into a different world. Tiny windows high up on the cliff face looked absurd.

Huge walled mountains surrounded three sides of the valley and I thought how perfect a location it was for paragliding, adding it to a never-ending list of places to fly my glider. To soar silently over this landscape would be an incredible experience.

I was becoming overloaded by unforgettable sights but knew I could not miss the fairy chimneys of Pasabag. I cringed at the mangy camel waiting patiently for tourists eager to capture an 'authentic' photo and longed to ride him away from his miserable existence. The chimneys stood unmoved as I sat in the snow with a Danish girl who couldn't stop giggling at their phallic like silhouettes.

Day two saw me making my way timidly towards Soganli valley on a rented scooter. I passed stark rock strewn valleys and miserable looking villages where men sat mummified in blankets gawking at nothing. Poverty was quite evident in this area, boys in rags sat on the icy roadside playing with their toes and thin old women were bent double with large sacks on their backs. Eventually I stopped to take in the sight before me. The immense cliff face ran for over a kilometre and was dotted chaotically with miniature windows which were once pigeon coups. The precious droppings were collected by local monks and used for centuries as crop fertilizer. I thought of Gaudi.

Cave churches were painstakingly dug from the hillside. There were neither tourists nor worshippers and I relished the silence as the world stood still. Small doorways were decorated with ancient red markings and pillars of various designs propped up fragile ceilings. I ducked low through an entrance way and was saluted by six colourful apostles. Many of these decorative frescoes had been sacrilegiously scrapped away but high above on the ceiling some have survived. I became dizzy as I twirled around gazing up at the powerful images. Jesus looked down solemnly as I ate my lunch.

I quickly visited the underground city of Derinkuyu. Areas for storage were initially carved out of the soft rock by the Hittites. At a much later period these were extended down to eight storeys by the Christians who sought refuge from the Romans and the Arabs before they became a legitimate religion. In the 14th Century, after the area was incorporated into the Ottoman Empire and the external threat abated, the underground cities were abandoned.

These enormous complexes could support a huge number of inhabitants for long periods of time and included wells, store rooms, stables, ventilation tunnels, wineries, kitchens and churches. As the temperatures outside either soared or declined well below minus, the temperature underground remained pleasant and perfect for storage.

Having head-butted the low ceilings several times I began to feel claustrophobic and disorientated so returned to my home above ground where I over indulged on *mussaka* and red wine.

Cappadocia had been so much more than I had hoped and although it was difficult to leave I knew I still had over two months of cycling ahead of me. The scenery became drab once more and I began to miss having company. I stopped to ask a dumbstruck teenager about a hotel. He groaned and raised both his hands in front of my face. This could have meant ten kilometres but I doubted this poor creature could count that high.

At a petrol station the gangly attendant spoke to me in Queen's English and agreed to let me share his office. The temperatures were now minus twenty at night and the lack of hotels meant I had no choice but to bunk down wherever I could find warmth. I was quite content though. Batur adjusted the glasses on his long nose and informed me in a modest whisper how he had a degree in International Relations. How absurd it was to have this articulate man who, unable to find an appropriate job, had resorted to pumping gas in order to support his wife and child. He was shy and nervous in total contrast to his lively work mate who, at thirty two, had acquired two wives and eleven children. We all agreed it was inevitable as he was a handsome man but I wondered about the children's prospects supported by only their father's measly wage.

Their boss arrived and we drank fresh warm milk from a large can. They were intrigued by *Bobby Sands*, whose struggle for freedom they could relate to. They could not conceive the idea of a voluntary cycle trip and repeatedly asked me why I had come to their ice-covered village in the desolate mountains of Central Turkey. I joked that I had come to find a wife which they all found dreadfully inappropriate and offensive. The conversation dwindled and we stared at an over dramatized love affair on TV. Batur offered me the use of his prayer beads and in reflex, I declined a little too hastily. He looked at the ground disappointed as he lit a cigarette.

The two couches were taken so they offered me a mattress sprawled on the oily floor of a store room. I was grateful although a little apprehensive that I may die of hypothermia. I pulled my ear warmers over my thermal face mask, my woolly hat over my ear warmers, my hood over my hat and said good night. I donned every piece of clothing I owned, lay down on the soggy mattress and pulled five blankets over my rain jacket. There were holes in the walls where pipes had once escaped but now invited in the ice cold air. I ducked under the blankets to do push ups in the hope of getting blood to circulate before passing out with exhaustion.

I awoke to a bright yellow room with sunlight shining through coloured glass. I tripped over large cans of motor oil, tumbled onto the greasy floor and sat bleary eyed looking at the filth in which I'd slept. I ripped away my layers of head coverings, pleased I had not succumbed to frostbite.

Batur was already running back and forth to the pumps as his workmate stood in his underwear warming his hands next to the stove, a towel wrapped around his head like a turban. A bus pulled alongside the window and he waved to shocked school girls before yawning and scratching himself.

The quiet road was shrouded in thick mist as I carefully manoeuvred between giant potholes. I glimpsed the occasional facade of a derelict house and trees emerged out of the eerie blur. The road climbed and I ate bananas with an old man who stood silently awestruck. He leaned on his cane, trembling with the cold. His neck strained to hold his heavy head, his eyes drooped and I failed to determine how or why he had come to be there.

The afternoon sun thawed the ground and sent up clouds of condensation. It was a magical performance and I yearned to share it with somebody. I began to think about a statement a friend of mine had recently asked my opinion on. She believed that an experience no matter how magnificent is entirely futile unless shared with a loved one. Although I had reservations about her belief, having spent over eight years travelling alone, I could nevertheless see how by sharing an experience it becomes all the more enjoyable. Of course you cannot force yourself to fall in love and without it life doesn't quite have the same appeal but to use this as an excuse not to seek out new experiences is to me wrong. Some believe if you have a strong connection with a person then you have a duty to work at the relationship in order for love to grow but I suppose I have always had a more romantic outlook. Love has however evaded me, so maybe I am the fool.

A head wind enjoyed teasing my weakened state, rightly punishing me for my wandering thoughts of loneliness and self pity. All day I'd been enjoying cheers and waves of encouragement as I toiled forward painfully slow. Railway workers beckoned me from their camp fire so I dismounted and went to thaw my hands. They were a group of three jibbering men and two obedient women. They patted the wooden plank on which they sat and I plonked my weary body down. The fire crackled and I used my ever expanding, although still quite pathetic, command of Turkish to explain who I was.

They cared little for my journey, more for my biscuits and the relief from monotony I provided. The men's hands and faces were stained black from mixing tar and even though they were good natured I could see hardship in their tired expressions. Their teeth were rotten with only a few hanging on precariously to red gums. I told a juvenile joke I'd learnt about fancying older women and they cracked up, slapping knees, back thumping and shrieking with laughter. Once the commotion subsided, the woman wearing a dark purple headscarf blew her nose into her hands and offered me a glass of tea.

As the sun went down the men stood in a little cleared area facing a red rock, marking Mecca, to perform their evening worship. The women whispered to each other before pulling their scarves tightly around their faces. My breath formed clouds of condensation, blurring my view and providing a welcome distraction. The men shouted for our attention and we shuffled off towards a collection of tin huts. The spindly women carried two of my bags each while the men laughed at my clumsiness. We stumbled along in the near dark through a field of human excrement lying frozen half sunk in a bed of snow.

Their hut was sparse with three sagging mattresses draped over metal spring frames. A large barrel of water had a plastic mug floating on the surface and we took turns washing our faces and spitting the water onto the compacted gravel floor. A naked bulb hung from a warped branch of a tree which supported the temporary roof. An ancient electric radiator was placed on top of a plastic crate mostly, I think, for of my admiration. I reclined listening to the gurgle and squeal of the warming element as they all went about their evening chores. I felt comfortable in their cosy home. They accepted me as an equal and I trusted them unconditionally.

I awoke to moonlight, drawn to the centre of the bed by the weight of a man who lay next to me, facing in the opposite direction. His feet were drawn up close to my face. His stubbly toes and the intricate pattern of his soles shone in the dim light. I shivered uncontrollably in countless layers but he snored happily in a worn out pair of shorts. He wheezed and shifted wildly, pushing me with his bulging stomach to the perimeter of our little mattress. Noise emanated from across the hut as springs strained and metal creaked in a rhythm. Words were muffled, grunts were released and urgent heavy breathing filled the silence. I smiled at the situations I find myself in and swore to find a hotel the following night.

Having put back on my cold dripping socks and wet boots I pedalled into the morning sun. Pairs of men moved along the road in slow motion, heads bowed. *Frankie Gavin* blasted in my ears as I passed three elderly women wearing brightly coloured baggy dresses, white flowing head scarves trailing in the breeze.

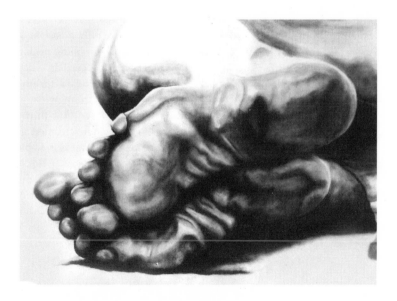

Nature's Magic and the Struggles of Man

A break at a *lokanta* with the most hideous turquoise interior imaginable saw me devouring an eggplant and mutton dish. I had become quite addicted to this food and searched it out whenever possible. In a quiet corner three unaccompanied females, two without headscarves, sat chatting and I found myself surprised by the unusual sight. The waiters paced like nervous monkeys in a cage. They waited impatiently eager to pounce on empty dishes. The women were all incredibly unattractive yet they were being ogled by the entire restaurant as if supermodels. Everyone froze mid chew to stare as they got up to leave.

The one continuous uninspiring line of the road cut through the icy terrain. I found myself singing aloud, a rare occurrence. Entering a hotel I discarded my beaten up bags on the floor and stood under the shower for a long time. I collapsed on the bed naked staring up at paintings of a tropical beach and a big bearded mullah.

My body was succumbing to the physical rigours. My nose was burnt from several days of bright sun combined with frostbite and felt as if it had been doused with acid. My chest had become painful. With every deep breath or twist of the body it felt as if cracked ribs poked into my lungs on the left side. Although deteriorating each day I hoped it would improve with the warmer weather only a couple of weeks away. My latest impediment was a stiff and throbbing neck. I guessed holding my head at a certain angle for long periods when cycling had damaged tendons. I could not look behind as turning more than a few inches to either side sent shockwaves from my ear to my lower neck muscles, mostly on the right side. I cycled with my head held upright, looking foolishly pompous. I often screamed as bumps and potholes caused me excruciating pain and not being able to look around was dangerous on busy roads.

I checked my email at reception and received a message from my mom idolizing a friend who had 'braved' a two week guided tour of Morocco.

Several days later a sense of regret came over me. The trip had become restricted by my desire to cover a minimum number of kilometres each day. I was missing out on experiences because I agonized over lost time as I pursued my quest of travelling eastwards with a zeal bordering on obsession. I have always resented routine and life revolving around time-tables but here I was, with all the freedom I could ask for, senselessly regimenting myself.

I was angry at how removed I had become from the people and places I was travelling through. Endless hours of tiring mountain roads and lack of companionship had left me feeling empty and uninterested. I yearned to rejuvenate the spontaneity and exhilaration of the moment. Before I could see sense, I steered the bike off the road and plummeted down a steep gravely slope. My heavily laden bike plunged into deep snow vaulting me over the handlebars. I tried to push myself upwards but only proceeded to make small tunnels.

I emerged shrieking from the ice cold pain but loving the adrenaline. I threw icy snow around, determined to rid myself of my dull demeanour. I lay on my back watching thin wispy clouds swim slowly across the blue sky. Emerging from my episode of madness I felt enthusiastic about embracing my carefree existence.

A dark smoky hall in Imranli was full of chatter. I sat watching an old man patiently turning *kofte* over an open fire. Young boys wearing tattered suit jackets, floppy hats and Wellington boots peered through misty glass and cajoled each other to approach the foreigner who had appeared out of the night. Teenagers sitting behind me were having a heated conversation and apparently wanted me to mediate. A phone was thrust into my hand, the screen showing a dead dog lying with mouth open on red stained snow. I was confused as one guy shouted irately. Had he shot somebody's dog in revenge or was he about to shoot some guy who had killed his dog? His eyes were blood shot and he was slightly deranged. The merry waiters dragged him away with apologies.

I took the morning off in order to explore some hidden villages high up in the hills above the town. A narrow road wound its way through deep banks of untouched snow and a hawk hovered high overhead. A young girl sat on the hood of a tractor brushing her hair as if in a trance. Dogs yanked at chains, unaccustomed to the intrusion.

Snow piled up to the roofs of dilapidated huts and concrete walls were succumbing to their heavy load. Life there must be unbearably difficult with the dominating mountainside seemingly determined to bury these people's homes.

Crows cawed and fighter jets boomed over head shattering the tranquillity. I sat drinking Ayran, a Turkish yogurt drink, and marvelled at the sweeping white meadows that stretched to the towering mountain peaks on the horizon. How cool I thought it would be to have my snowboard and drift down through the untouched powder to the town far below.

Later that day I climbed slowly to the highest pass so far at 2190 metres. The slopes glistened silver, my nose shone red and snow stung my eyes. I strained to catch my breath but enjoyed the feeling of my strong leg muscles propelling me up the steep gradient.

The phrase, 'Ne Mutlu Turkum Diyene' (Proud is the one who can call himself a Turk), along with a crescent and moon (symbols of the Turkish nationhood) were painted on rocksides. These were intended to remind rebellious Kurds of their patronage and screamed of intolerance.

Several days of monotonous hills and lack of mental stimulus saw me pedalling along hypnotized by the dirt two metres ahead of my front wheel. My mind flitted over past events and future dreams but soon my trail of thought was lost. I craved something unusual to happen and extract me from my tedium. Whatever God exists must have been listening as from around a tight corner came an army jeep with machine gun mounted on the back. The vehicle slowed and the helmeted man who stood at the weapon turned to look at me suspiciously before vanishing as quickly as he had appeared. I had also turned to stare and had inadvertently drifted across the road, not realizing there were more vehicles to follow. An eight-wheeled tank with a huge menacing canon trundled directly at me and I nearly went into the coffee stained river as I swerved to avoid this ominous monster. It stopped, hissed and squeaked as I pedalled slowly by, unsure what the men secured inside were thinking. I continued further along the steep sided canyon expecting to confront more army vehicles but to my disappointment I remained alone with my thoughts.

8

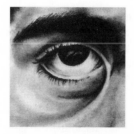

Haggling Burqas, Hassling Bakers and a Sad Chef

One evening at an internet café in a nondescript town, I was amazed to see every computer screen displaying pornography. Groups of young men paced up and down admiring one fornicating woman after another. They cheered and clapped in encouragement as I attempted to compose an email to my mom. Many came up behind me and pointed at the screen as if shocked to see mere lettering and not bouncing breasts. Kerry had just beaten Derry in the league.

I regard myself as being no different from the vast majority of Irish men who during the years of adolescence was keen on pornography. However, as the years go by and one becomes more sexually experienced, porn becomes less appealing and rather redundant. These guys, ranging from their late teens to early forties, lacked an outlet for their sexual curiosity thus flocking to the World Wide Web. Their exposure to the West was also very limited. Looking daily at voluptuous blondes eagerly performing every sexual act imaginable, one can understand why they then assumed that the entire Western population is thus inclined. Back in reality they walk down a street where an occasional aloof female ambles by, head bowed, with only hands and sometimes face exposed – a different creature from those females who inhabit the fantastic world of porn.

I went in search of a shop to satisfy my ice cream craving, in one freezer I found chickens, in another there was ice. I made a fist and.

pretended to lick it creating howls of laughter. One good humoured man led me up the street by the arm. He shouted to his friends what I imagined to be, 'Hey look at this crazy Irish comedian. He is looking for an ice cream,' chuckling at his own wit.

They responded, 'Doesn't he know it's minus five degrees? But hey, we have nothing better to do than think about porn so let's go with him.'

Our expanding group resembled a mini demonstration as we blocked traffic and shooed away hungry pigs that scavenged in the gutter. We stormed into an identical shop and interrupted the feeble owner from his prayers. He was overwhelmed by the excitement but managed to spread an assortment of tubs and cones on the counter for all to see. The group had attracted more onlookers fascinated by the commotion. Guys pushed and shoved, desperate for a better view. I was pinned to the counter and heard a pile of washing powder boxes crash to the floor.

I chose the biggest tub of chocolate ice cream available, creating a wave of excitement amongst the assembly. We piled out onto the street with me juggling the freezing tub in my bare hands. The conversation went along a familiar path. Robbie Keane was Ireland's only known person, the young men here being as obsessed with football as anywhere else in the world. The second, a little disconcertingly, was the IRA. They were known as Western Europe's equivalent of the PKK and thus applauded in these parts. I wondered if the two groups had affiliations. The third was usually whiskey although no brand names were ever forthcoming. I thought if these three things were my country's greatest contribution to humanity, should I not be ashamed?

Sitting on steps I watched the crowd of sniffing kids and groggy men, who simultaneously watched my every move. Two boys leaned over my shoulder and it took me a few seconds to realize why. I often leave my Ipod on and my earphones dangling around my neck, not wanting to remove myself from reality but still able to hear the music. I presented one to each. They jumped around behind me in excitement, arms and legs flailing to a *Dervisch* jig. I doubted they would have been so enthusiastic had they known how badly they had done in the Eurovision.

Guys encouraged me to eat the ice cream as my red woolly hat was passed around. I scraped timidly at the solid block with a flimsy plastic spoon. I passed the tub around but everyone declined until I caught one guy in a headlock and forcefed him, leaving the poor fella humiliated with a brown sticky face. The crowd were in hysterics and magically a proper spoon was found. A chubby kid walked around with the tub held proudly above his head like a trophy as everyone took turns digging in.

A large tray of tea arrived which tasted suspiciously like paraffin. Our gathering resembled a *ceilí* with free booze held at a social welfare office. I changed the music to Michael Jackson for some variety. This induced convulsions from my grinning ten year old dance fans. They gyrated and thrust their hips inappropriately only inches from the back of my head. I dared not look behind, yet thought how approving Mr Jackson would be if he could see the comical scene.

The weather deteriorated and several days later I arrived in Erzurum soaked to the skin. I spent hours cleaning clothes before venturing out to the Iranian embassy. An arc of muddy water from a truck made me regret even attempting to seem presentable. For the first time the majority of women wore the all enveloping black *burqa*.

I noticed postcards for sale depicting army personnel proudly posing, with 'Commando' brazenly printed at the top. These were popular with young army recruits who sent them home to parents while doing their military service. The hype surrounding young men's initiation into adulthood was to me sad and unnecessary. To teach adolescents how to kill as an introduction to maturity seemed totally contradictory.

Military compounds lined the road and I waved to groups of recruits doing their morning exercises. Police escorted columns of military vehicles. Light armoured jeeps were followed by lorries with rows of soldiers, their faces painted in camouflage and guns at the ready. Huge canons were pulled by trucks driven by Rambo lookalikes. Sparkling clean tanks, both wheeled and caterpillared, rattled by, Turkish flags flapping from their aerials.

I passed several extremely poor settlements where children played in piles of rubbish and plates of cow dung dried in the sun. I walked around several villages to give my backside a rest, admiring the butcher shop, the café and the doctor's office, all the while feeling like the Pied Piper, as gangs of inquisitive children seemed to find me a hysterical form of entertainment. The entire male population of one village seemed to be out in the muddy streets mingling with horses, sheep, tractors and generally making a festive mess.

Women herded cattle from barren mountain slopes. Kids sprinted down slippery tracks and tripped over themselves in their eagerness to reach the road before I passed. One boy emerged onto the road triumphant but stood awkwardly unsure at what to do next. I stopped and shared a packet of biscuits with these adorable little fellas and wished I could take one away to keep me company. I anguished over leaving them with their faces distraught with sorrow and abandonment.

There were regular military checkpoints and at one I was asked for my first bribe. The smirking officer's beard was neatly trimmed. Mine was not. He displayed his perfect teeth and refused to let go of my hand. I pulled away but only managed to bring the arrogant man to within kissing distance. He smelled of sardines and his eyes were chocolate brown. He barked at the static on his radio and pretended to wait for a response. He was proud of his gadget and was determined to show it off. On realizing that he couldn't get anything from me, he cracked a joke at my expense in the hope of redeeming his hurt ego in front of his comrades.

At another checkpoint, on top of a large mountain pass, the officer was more cordial. We joked together in English while surrounded by twelve soldiers. Three pairs held hands. They mostly looked like impoverished farmers, fondled their antique rifles clumsily and whispered amongst themselves. The senior officer was quite a character and joked about his useless soldiers. They appeared impressed.

Curious Companions

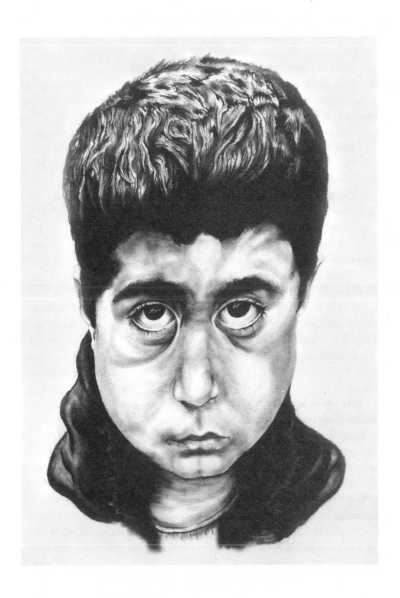

'What is your education sir?' He began a confusing interrogation.

'University,' I lied.

'Your job?'

'Ahh Manager,' I half lied.

'You are terrorist?'

I laughed and smacked a young lad on the back. 'No, no sir. Tourist not terrorist.'

The men echoed my statement as if it were a profound thought. 'Married?'

'No.' Progressively getting more truthful.

'You like my gun?'

'Oh yes, very impressive.' It looked like an air rifle to me.

'You like killing English?'

'There are troubles in my country as in yours.'

'We like killing infidels,' he grinned and received a cheer from the pensive crowd.

'There are bad people everywhere but I'm lucky to have met good people today,' I ventured.

'I will not kill you. You are my brother.' There seemed to be no middle ground between brother and enemy. 'You will marry my daughter. Is ugly girl. Good for you.'

I actually felt complimented. 'Inshallah, Inshallah' (Its Gods will), I said, seriously hoping Allah (Peace be upon Him) was not listening.

My weak legs shook as I neared Dogubayzit. My enthusiasm was deflated, my energy non-existent. I lay on gravel as mist blew over stark fields and a man wheeled a barrow through a muddy yard. Several villages of low lying houses were deserted, examples of the destruction caused by the conflict. I passed more checkpoints where I put my head down, knowing I would merely be used for my entertainment value. I would not be taken advantage of any longer. Their whistles slowly dwindled as they had no transport in which to follow.

Within a day I had come from snow clad mountains, to brown interlocking valleys where only thin strips of stubborn ice hid from the sun. Small patches of pale green were beginning to appear and I welcomed the warm breeze. Rock faces merged from turquoise to

Curious Companions

terracotta to purple. Women in vibrant dresses spread manure and kids sat on stone walls reminding me of Connemara. The silhouette of Mt Ararat's twin peaks dominated the horizon.

Small enthusiastic boys shined shoes for men going for their Friday visit to the mosque. Their faces glowed as they rubbed with all their might, delighted with the few coins they received. Several women begged for alms, their head scarves tightly wrapped around their faces, ashamedly hiding their identity. Old men sat crumpled on the pavement with prayer hats held out, benefiting from people's sympathy.

I had been told about zakat by Ozgur in Ankara and was impressed. He explained it as an Islamic act of purification when people give away something dear to them (money), resulting in self mortification thus diminishing their pride. It can be seen as a type of guilt relief for the more affluent donor and also makes the poor less envious of the rich. The needy are also released from the humiliation of pleading for charity by the belief that the rich give to Allah Himself, who then bestows the donation on the poor.

I liked the concept of this type of alms-giving. In reality, however, it was obvious the system had broken down. I looked around me at the destitute people pleading for charity, having long forgotten about religious protocol.

Cafés were full of arguments and laughter. Tea glasses were topped up, men dozed and smoke hung defiant. A man with blotchy skin on his face leaned in close and whispered about an incident in 1993 when a PKK unit executed thirty unarmed military recruits. He taught me the saying, 'çi bextewar e yê ku dibêje ez Kurd im' (happy is he who calls himself a Kurd), a common act of rebellion against the ideology of the Turkish State.

Men lined up with mats outside the overflowing mosque and caused a gridlock. They wore their best clothes with pride and knelt next to one another, shoulder to shoulder, in submission without class or status. Could this be a reason why so many of the world's poorest and most destitute turn to Islam, I wondered.

I loaded my bike before daybreak and had breakfast in a small *pastanesi*. The over-weight man behind the counter wore lazy eyelids and yawned. I was the only customer and enjoyed my cakes and tea until the baker sat down opposite. The chair creaked under the pressure of his bulk. I sipped, he stared. He rubbed a chubby finger over an oily nose and told me how he was an expert masseuse. He lit a cigarette, placed a hand on my leg and urged me to accompany him to the public *hamam*. I laughed at his forwardness and told me I would prefer to eat the overflowing ashtray. He either did not understand or refused to acknowledge the rejection.

'Are you a religious man?' I began, wanting to know his view on homosexuality in Islam.

'Of course, "There is no God but Allah and Muhammad is His prophet." ' He chuckled and continued to scratch his crotch like a diseased dog.

'I thought homosexuality was forbidden in Islam,' I said feeling very uncomfortable but determined not to let him know it.

'Yes you correct sir. I am not homosexual. You are wrong.'

'In my country a man who is attracted to men is a homosexual,' I explained.

'I not homosexual. I like fuck man and boys but homosexual is forbidden.' He sat back in his chair with legs widely spread as I agonized over where to look.

I thought uneasily about the hundreds of frustrated men I had met from many different societies who, with women out of sight, out of touch until marriage, resorted to gay sex while refusing to admit any homosexual tendencies. I believed Islam to probably be the most rigidly anti-homosexual of all the world religions. There are no debates as to its legality just about the severity of the punishment.

Dr. Muzammil Siddiqi of the ISNA (Islamic Society of North America) is reported to have said, 'Homosexuality is a moral disorder. It is a moral disease, a sin and corruption... No person is born homosexual, just like no one is born a thief, a liar or murderer. People acquire these evil habits due to a lack of proper guidance and education.'

Wherever a person believes homosexuality originates, this blatant bigotry and spread of hatred should not be condoned in any society. Although also similarly condemned by other religions, one cannot ignore the shocking estimates that say 4,000 homosexuals have been executed in Iran since the revolution in 1979.

I was trying to remain impartial. Thankfully I had been brought up to believe in respect and tolerance. Like the vast majority of young Irish people, I believe that as long as it is not unavoidably thrust in your face, people's sexual orientation is their own business. Homosexuality in the context of a consenting relationship between two adults seems perfectly acceptable to me. Where I object is when men turn to sex with vulnerable young men and boys out of desperation. As my aroused breakfast associate demonstrated this is often accepted as a social norm.

Garbage men stared in dismay at the muddy street. A lone foreign girl walked by, agitated by two guys wearing baseball caps who called out to her. She carried a water bottle for fear of dehydration.

Arriving at the Iranian border I chatted with a security guard who applauded my Turkish, before I yet again began a new language. I negotiated the persistent money changers and tourist guides and sped down the dusty hill into Iran. The vast majority of signs were in the perplexing Persian alphabet and I searched for somewhere resembling a bank.

I entered a lowrise building and came face to face with a stunned crowd. The twenty or so men had taken a pause from their shouting to stare but to my relief soon began again. The place resembled a nightclub five minutes before closing, where a group of unruly drunks try desperately to get a last drink. They crowded around the counter shouting, pushing and waving wads of notes in despair. Decorum was non-existent as the patient teller served whoever had the determination to thrust their cash in his face with the most aggression. I joined the scrum a little hesitantly at first with apologies and excuse me's, but before long found myself dragging and pushing smiling farmers out of my way. They seemed to enjoy the competitiveness of the experience. With one transaction completed the melee surged forward. The inevitably defeated men jibber jabbered and the process began again. I reached the counter within a respectable twenty minutes and harassed the stone faced clerk who whispered, 'no exchange money.'

I hated nothing more than retracing my steps, so continued unsure where I might exchange money as international Credit Cards were not accepted here. Cars had little concern for rules but drivers hooted and waved eagerly. Ominous dark thunder clouds filled the horizon and lightening fizzled downwards. A deluge began, rain falling in heavy sheets. Staring at the puddles on the road and listening to the patter of rain on my hood made me think of home.

That night saw me touring an almost deserted hotel that hadn't seen a customer in over a month. Its weariness was almost charming. The owner was a weasel-like man with a lopsided grin and wore a woman's overcoat with padded shoulders. He explained in detail how the window could be used to let in fresh air, demonstrated the use of a light switch and told me that he had hung a towel next to the door so people would see it and be able to use it. My host took me by the hand to a kebab shop in a narrow covered lane where I devoured meat and rice as he explained the positives and negatives of concrete and rubber.

The streets were awash with drifting burqas as crowds went about shopping for the upcoming No Ruz (Iranian New Year). They haggled enthusiastically with their arms, voices muffled by the cloth covering their mouths. It felt unnerving being engulfed by these mysterious gliding figures. They regularly stared at me in surprise before pulling the cloth closer around their faces in humiliation. They acted as if I had degraded them with my eyes and I felt bad for causing their discomfort.

I knew the Koran advises modesty, instructing women to 'lower their gazes and be mindful of their chastity'. Women are directed to 'draw their head covering over their bosoms', except in the presence of immediate family. The Prophet Mohamed's son-in-law, Ali ibn Taleb, the first Shiite leader, wrote, 'Almighty God created sexual desire in ten parts, then he gave nine parts to women and one to men.' Muslim theologians advocate the segregation of men and women because they believe desire is a force so powerful that the faithful must be protected from it. The veiling of women has manifested itself out of this distrust of female sexuality.

The attitude in the West of being adverse to women's coverings, I feel, is a reaction against the supposed suppression of women's rights. However, voluntary female modesty as a form of self protection is most common and after centuries of conditioning it seems a mistake to say these women's rights are being suppressed. Head scarves are not unknown even amongst the liberated women of the West and the possibility that the wearer may herself wish to follow the injunctions of the Koran as to personal modesty, are often ignored.

Charlie Chaplin observed that every man, on encountering an eligible female, calculates even if only momentarily, what his prospects may be. The real core of the issue surely originated from men's relentless pursuit of the opposite sex. Was it the case that appropriate codes of conduct could not be instilled on rogue men and therefore a greater restriction on women had to be imposed? To me it is a woman's right to protect herself from the unwanted attention of longing egotistical men. I had asked the question countless times over the past month regarding the need for women's coverings. Without exception the men believed Muslim women were so precious that they were obligated to protect and guard them. None admitted to the need for protection stemming from men's uncontrollable desires. The burqa, I premise, is one of the ways in which men try to shield their loved ones from the big bad world and I believe will never be accepted by the West's 'equality' society.

I bought fruit which Mr Weasel adamantly replaced with his own carefully selected samples. After a thorough door locking practice session and a conversation about the different pronunciation between chicken and kitchen the infuriating chipmunk finally left me in a heavenly silence.

The attention I received as I carried on towards Marand was heart warming. I waved to young shepherds and stopped to talk with road workers. They thanked me profusely for taking their photos as we posed beside a truck pumping out black rancid smoke. Kids delighted in trying to snap the gear cables on my bike and screeched when I chased them away.

The large burly men joked and laughed in a childlike way without what seemed like a care in the world. They possessed neither jealousy nor resentment towards their place in life. They spent their days shovelling earth and breaking rocks by hand but were assured, by their beliefs, that this was where they were meant to be. I asked them if they enjoyed their work and they responded with, 'La hawala wala quwwata illa billah' (There is no power but that of Allah) – basically everyone is powerless in the hands of God's will. They believed they had no say over their destinies, subsequently worry, displeasure or resistance was pointless. If a person is born into poverty then it is God's will and must be endured. This concept, that one should accept their place in society and not strive to better one's circumstance, conflicts heavily with my own opinions of equal opportunity and an obvious reason why so many millions of poor are easily exploited.

Marand is a large town. I found the one and only hotel on the outskirts. I cringed as I neared the Tourist Inn but decided I was badly in need of a wash. The morose receptionist ordered money from me, shouting indignantly in Farsi as if I were deaf. I happily thought of Johnny in Alexandria. I struggled up the steps with my bike draped over one shoulder and two bags in each hand as the bag boy shouted, 'come on, come on with bicycle inside.' He stood back from the glass door with a smirk, so I kicked it open with a loud clatter, disappointed it didn't smash. The place was sterile and uninspiring so after a long soak to rid myself of layers of dirt, I hopped into a taxi in the direction of town.

I joined the throngs of shoppers, bought an enormous bag of dried fruit and entered the relative seclusion of a restaurant. Old men argued with a young Turk over visa applications. Their ID cards were antique slips of frayed paper from the time of the *Shah*.

The chef joined me as I filled my rumbling belly. I scooped up sloppy omelette with hunks of flattened bread as a cigarette danced between his lips to the rhythm of his talk. He was a proud Kurd and decided I was worthy of the truth regarding the treatment of his people in Iran. The Kurds as in Turkey are Sunni Muslim and have been persecuted by the Shia central establishment in Tehran.

After the creation of Iran, the Kurds, with their different language, traditions and cross-border allegiances, were seen by the *Ayatollah Khomeini* as vulnerable to exploitation by foreign powers, who wished to destabilize the young Republic. 'Sometimes the word minorities is used to refer to people such as Kurds, Lurs, Turks, Persians, Baluchis, and such,' he stated. 'These people should not be called minorities, because this term assumes that there is a difference between these brothers. In Islam, such a difference has no place at all. There is no difference between Muslims who speak different languages, for instance, the Arabs or the Persians. It is very probable that such problems have been created by those who do not wish Muslim countries to be united.... They create the issues of nationalism... and such-isms which are contrary to Islamic doctrines. Their plan is to destroy Islam and Islamic philosophy.'

By tying all of his people to Islam the country's leader, time and again, accused foreign powers of attacking their faith where often purely economic factors or distrust within his own people were to blame.

As early as 1979 armed conflict broke out between Kurdish factions and the Iranian government's security forces. I had read that mobile revolutionary courts were set up under the supervision of infamous Islamic judges like Ayatollah Khalkhali, who sentenced thousands of men to execution after summary trials, without regard for the rights of the accused. Those executed included civilians, suspected Kurdish fighters and sympathizers of other armed opposition groups who centred their military operations in the mountainous Kurdish region.

During the war between Iran and Iraq, armed Kurdish political groups refused to align themselves against their own government but neither would they fight their own kinsmen from across the border. This lack of allegiance has condemned the Kurds to poverty from lack of development, as well as military action. The civilian population has been a major victim of the conflict with more than two hundred and seventy Kurdish villages being destroyed and depopulated between 1980 and 1992.

My chef was sceptical of bringing about change through a political route. Not surprising, as Kurdish political leaders have been the targets of political assassinations by the government inside and outside Iran. According to Kurdish opposition groups, the government deals with Kurdish political organisations through arbitrary detention, torture and the execution of prisoners after 'unfair trials'. He was now extremely despondent. Great strain and regret were etched in his face. He cursed the *Pasdaran* units whom he claimed forced Kurdish women to enter into temporary marriage contracts with them. The practice of temporary marriage, sanctioned within Shia Islamic custom but abhorrent to Sunni Muslims, constitutes a form of rape when carried out by force. His gaze dropped low, his voice trembled with emotion as he explained how his own sister had been a victim.

Back at the hotel I interrupted the bag boy who was arguing with his wife. He pushed her hard in the head and raised his hand as the petrified woman cowered like a scared dog. He saw me approaching and drew a swift kick at his surrendering wife. He smiled at me as if to demonstrate his authority. She got timidly into the rear of the car and they drove off with screeching tyres.

I had conflicting ideas about how I 'should' handle such a situation. Morally there is no question I would have intervened and stopped this man's cruel and callous behaviour but I knew I had to be careful about interfering where I did not belong. Although the vast majority of Iranian men would also condemn violent behaviour towards women, I was somewhat sceptical of men possessing absolute power over their wives, who must accept their word without question. For an outsider to tell a Muslim man how he can or can't treat his wife is considered completely unacceptable. I had been prepared to embrace people's beliefs and systems but when they directly contradicted my own basic morals I found it difficult to ignore. Was this considerate or cowardly on my part? Who knows. Surely there is a limit to one's tolerance beyond which injustice can no longer be ignored.

9

Around and About with Ruffians

A few quick sunny hours ride through dry windswept hills with red outcrops saw me arrive in Tabriz with an equally bright red nose. Streets were cluttered with impatient traffic manoeuvring around temporary stalls and stubborn dogs. I dragged my bicycle through huge crowds to a cheap crumbling hovel of a hotel.

A stall sold delicious warm bread served with fresh cream and natural honey. I sat on a fragile stool and enjoyed the local breakfast with two local *Azari* men who wore baggy trousers that any raver would envy. The pavement was taken up with displays of all kinds of goods imaginable. Metal containers were filled with gold fish, women fought through mounds of bras, young boys sold packets of sweets and old men got swept away in the chaos.

I explored the labyrinth of bazaars, apparently thirty five kilometres of them, dodging carts and hanging ornaments. The narrow alleyways were crammed with scrummaging shoppers. I trod repeatedly on lose trailing black cotton and apologized to ghost-like individuals. Gentle carpet sellers bought me tea which I sipped cautiously from a saucer, having placed a sugar cube between my teeth. They detested America who they claimed were 'very big terrorists', although I'm sure they would have treated them with the same respect as they did me if they had been there to acquire carpets instead of oil. They believed a combined Iranian-Palestinian attack would devastate the United States in the year 2009. This was the beginning of constant misgivings about the US I would encounter over the following month.

They believed their faith was being demonized by the West. It saddened me how susceptible people are to negative opinions just as I'd seen with anti-Islamic sentiments back home. Even though my family and friends knew little about Iran it caused more concern than any other country I had planned to visit.

These men looked back to when America first began intruding in Iran's policies. The reasons were political and economic, America needing Iran as an ally against bordering Soviet Union during the Cold War and also for their supply of oil. In order to foster popular support at home for their actions, the process of demonizing Islam by labelling it 'fundamentalist' and 'revolutionary' was undertaken.

The Ayatollah Khomeini labelled the United States, the 'Great Shaytan' (Satan), because of their support of the deeply corrupt ruling Shah. He suppressed the popular religious life of the people, in the name of modernization. To Khomeini, the Shah and his Western backers were working against God's law, thus allying themselves with the devil. All this from the man who subsequently reduced the age at which women could marry to nine and who sent waves of young men to their death on the Iraqi front, by persuading them they would go straight to paradise as martyrs.

Understandably these carpet sellers felt angered by the challenge the West poses to Islam, as an alternative source of values and social organization which endangers their traditional ways. They reiterated the opinion that each encroachment by the US-dominated world produces the reaction of a greater commitment among Muslims to their code. 'The God-sent light of Islam will never give way to secular materialism,' one said (or something of the sort in a combination of languages and hand signs) wagging a freshly rolled cigarette at me and cackling for reasons he alone knew.

They sympathized with me for having to live in such an immoral society. Their view was that Westerners who transgress the rules of God, are punished by having to endure a world wrought with destructive behaviour, such as increased crime, lack of family values,

large rates of drug and alcohol abuse and single parent families. I opted not to tell them that I overindulged in alcohol for many years, frequently enjoy sex outside of marriage and my parents were recently divorced.

I agreed with my reactionary friends that my mother would delight in receiving a new handmade four metre long carpet, but alas thought it a little impractical to strap one to my bicycle. I defied balloon sellers and artificial flower hawkers and gave my change to someone squatting under a cloak resembling a large bundle of clothes.

The following day became an ordeal. Heat increased seemingly by the minute and I agonized over not finding a minute of privacy. Weakness overcame me in waves. I lay on a pile of rubble and cursed the groups of young men who stopped to enquire about my wellbeing.

As I began to wonder where to rest my head for the night two teenagers on a coughing motorbike paused to examine me. I was very much an object of curiosity in those parts. They were outraged that there was no hotel in their hometown of Malakan and easily convinced me to spend the night with them.

We entered through the tall walled exterior of Hedayat's home and into the inner sanctuary of a small courtyard. Plain mud packed walls such as these dominated the townscape, forbidding the gaze of outsiders. I was ushered inside the main room where his mother welcomed me warmly. I deposited myself on the carpeted floor and was immediately plied with tea and dried fruits. Zeinab, Hedayat's fifteen year old sister, busied herself in the kitchen and smiled at me self-consciously from under the brim of her *hijab*. She was tall and attractive and obviously unused to the company of strange men. She fidgeted nervously with her long black flowing gown and passively accepted the orders of her mother and impatient brother. I felt uneasy as she poured tea, prepared food, put on a DVD for us, answered the door, then the telephone, cleaned up and looked after her hyperactive little sister. I disliked Hedayat's demanding and unappreciative attitude but understood that families assign much importance to the authority of the eldest son.

Zahra was the youngest of the family and enjoyed the attention focused on her. Although only eight she was also forced to wear a head scarf in my presence, something she did not take kindly to. Several times she was reprimanded for revealing her hair, no doubt compromising her decency in front of a stranger.

The room was simply decorated with a thick carpet but no furniture. A painting of *Imam* Reza hung next to a large photo of a waterfall with posing deer. I felt pleased that the women of the family had begun to relax in my company, Zeinab practising her English with me and Zahra relishing her new playmate.

I was surprised when a DVD of Turkish music was put on. A long legged woman wearing not much more than a bikini pranced around on stage shaking her breasts to the beat. Zahra of course jumped about in reckless gaiety, copying the pouting lips of the singer and surprisingly her mother merely looked on mutely. This was surely a negative influence on young impressionable adolescents. The girls were not permitted to show their forearms in public and gazed admiringly at a woman who displayed her body explicitly.

With Dawood, a fifteen year old lunatic as our driver, we went for a 'scenic tour'. We three squeezed onto the motorbike and raced around town to satisfy these poor adrenaline junkies craving for danger. We lurched from side to side down crowded streets at an insane speed, skimming past oncoming cars, scattering chickens and leaving behind cursing old men in clouds of smoke.

They slowed slightly to stare longingly at girls who wore anything but long black burqas. A loosely fitting green outfit with flowery headscarf was comparable to a short skirt and low cut top, receiving admiring gazes from men, as well as disapproving glares from women. I was paraded around town like a trophy before we stopped to talk to a gruff man with evil eyes. Oscar had a scar running the length of his left cheek and a very large chip on his shoulder. He did not try to hide his contempt for me. He ordered me off the bike and with my back to a wall began barking questions in Farsi. He was dogmatic, refusing to believe I was a tourist. I was interrogated as a crowd grew around us. I surprised myself with how at ease I felt and laughed as he demanded money. My friends were nearing hysterics, pleading with their neighbour to stop the harassment. I thought it quite possible I might feel a blade in my side or at least the crack of a head butt at any second. He placed his hand on the wall behind my head, leaned in close and whispered what was no doubt a warning to leave town or else.

I had anticipated encountering a certain amount of hostility but was interested to know where his deep rooted hatred had originated. Did it stem from the Iran-Iraq war where America (thus any white foreigner) backed their enemy and hundreds of thousands of Iranians lost their lives? Did he despise the West for demonizing his most sacred religion? Did he resent my freedom or was he jealous of my supposed wealth? Or did he really suspect me of being some kind of spy? I put my hand out for him to shake but he continued with his provocative tirade of accusations.

Thankfully still alive, we reclined once again on Hedayat's living room floor as he, quite obviously shaken, recounted our recent adventures to his dad, while apologizing profusely to me. The evening's main meal was an elaborate affair with scores of exotic dishes laid out on a plastic sheet on the floor. We ate quickly with our hands. The women hovered nearby and served, only refraining with the most elaborate of protests. The father was a quiet bear like man who implored me to eat more. My hands were stained with the rich flavours of mutton curry and chicken kebab and I pleaded for mercy.

As us men sprawled with full bellies and drank tea, the women happily sat at one corner eating the leftovers. Zahra was becoming a handful and enjoyed sitting alongside me playing with a furry toy I had given her. She was innocently playful but I could feel her mother's disapproving eye, uncomfortable with a male outsider being in such close contact with her young daughter. I nodded as if in reassurance that I meant no harm as Zahra bound into my lap and threw her arms around my neck.

Endlessly curious family and friends arrived to observe me lounge on the carpet while I dreamt of being on a secluded island of beds. Whenever a male entered we all stood to attention in their honour and repeated the tedious exhibition of greetings and introductions. When a man left we took part in a similar display. I went to the bathroom and on returning the congregation rose to welcome me back. I thanked everyone for their concerns as my toilet breaks were discussed at length. I was tired of being the centre of attention and feeling the pressure of having to entertain. A baby was produced and thrust into my arms. It drooled on my arm as the women ohhed and ahhed and beamed smiles.

Mercifully, blankets were prepared for sleep. Hedayat dragged me outside where a gang of friends waited in a beat-up old car. We careened recklessly through the empty streets, nine of us packed tightly inside, the horn blared, we shouted and banged the sides of the car wildly. The skinny guy squashed against the driver's door operated the steering wheel, the fella next to him reached for the pedals and another fumbled with the gear stick. We bottomed out several times, sending sparks flying in the night. We stopped to pick up another friend who sat on the boot nonchalantly smoking a cigarette before finally coming to an abrupt halt in a deserted wasteland. A campfire was lit and we crouched on our haunches drinking putrid illegal liquor out of a plastic bag. They were a rough-looking, rowdy bunch but I was accepted unconditionally with kisses on both cheeks and firm handshakes. They were curious about Ireland and I answered questions repeatedly dispelling images of near naked women cruising the streets of Dublin in Ferraris begging men to get laid. I feigned delight as mobile phones with shockingly graphic pornography were passed around and I sympathized with their sexual frustration.

For some years I had foolishly believed the commonly held philosophy that living in a sexually repressed Islamic country provokes a mixture of rage and envy towards the permissive West. Some people had irrationally warned me that it leads to distorted, sexually frustrated personalities who can be prone to violence. The truth I came to realize is that the Catholic belief system, with regards to sex, is not so different from the Islamic one. What is different however, is how we adhere to that system. How religion itself is observed within our societies could not be more dissimilar, thus the reason behind our contrasting realities. The stringently observed code of Islamic countries, not so dissimilar to the strict Catholic society of my grandparent's generation, as compared to today's Irish society that seemingly continues its façade of faith for fear of controversy or insult.

What I had failed to understand was the fact that repression, according to Freud, is not the temporary abstinence from an instinctive act, but believing that the instinctive act is itself wrong. What Islam requires of young people is to control their passions without repressing them, to control them willingly and consciously, until the time of marriage. This sounds very similar to the principles I had once been taught.

A large percentage of the young men I met however, were unable to exercise their restraint, surrendering to the temptation of prostitution.

They told me gruesome stories of lining up to take turns on an obese woman who covered her head in shame and of picking up women as old as their mothers and ugly and wrinkled as their grandmothers and handing over several days of hard earned savings in order to satisfy their passions. This to me is the reality that stems from suppressing one's instinctive desires, the degradation of oneself out of frustration and desperation. To have sex with anyone but a prostitute would condemn them to, at the very least, a severe beating and at worst, an execution.

They craved to go to a disco so we danced around the flames to the sound of a ring tone, clapping, finger clicking and whooping into the still night. What a shame dancing is forbidden in public as these guys really ripped up our dusty dance floor.

Three hours later I was woken and suddenly found myself plodding down the still dark street with another group of Hedayat's friends, this time six eccentrically dressed sixteen year olds. One wore a dickie-bow and stained white shirt, looking as if he had just finished work at a restaurant. Another had huge flared jeans, a natural curly afro and freaky painted on eyebrows. A scrawny chap wore his younger sisters yellow top which clung to his bony body, revealing small whirls of blonde hair around his belly button.

We made our way with bleary eyes towards the river where several hundred people had already congregated. It was the morning of No Ruz and time for the Iranian festival of fire, Chahârshanbe Sûrî or Red Wednesday. This firework festival is the celebration of light (the good) winning over darkness (the bad).

I had experienced the excitement of Diwali (the festival of light) in India several times but as we strolled nearer this began to feel more like suburban warfare than a celebration. There was pandemonium as large crackers were lobbed at our heads and fireworks whizzed past, deafening us. Being the only foreigner I came in for the most attention. Several of the more unruly guys threw handfuls of crackers in retaliation and a bunch of miniature explosives were thrust into my pocket for self defence. A grenade sized projectile hit my neck, scalding the skin and blew up next to my hand, leaving me gasping in pain but which I concealed from my comrades.

Curious Companions

We sought safety in the crowd as a policeman, bombarded by fireworks, took refuge in a passing truck. Women bending low by the water's edge shrieked in panic as explosions splashed the water around them. A banger was placed in the rear of a car resulting in the driver knocking over two grinning pedestrians. A group circling a bonfire took turns jumping through the flames. People clapped and sang a song which I later learned was to banish their bad health. Rockets were shot at cowering crowds as men shielded the faces of their young. The sun began to illuminate the chaotic scene and flashes of sparks continued to rain down as we retreated.

It was six thirty and we sat on a street corner with a mentally disturbed man who drooled on his apron. Blaseen, a friend and energetic fish seller with a vibrant personality arrived. He believed our friendship was fate and we laughed at our inability to communicate. He resorted to a physical display of affection, kissing me on the cheek and hugging me to his smelly body so often that anywhere else in the world I would have felt indecently assaulted. Having grown up in a society where men are not encouraged to show physical affection towards each other, it took some time to feel comfortable with so much touching. It seemed that due to the lack of interaction with the opposite sex these teenagers concentrated all their affection on their male friends. Hands were placed on knees, fingers rubbed necks, cheeks were pinched and arms were slung comfortingly over shoulders. I was sure that if the lads from back home had seen me then they would no doubt have thought I had changed my sexual orientation. No matter how hard I tried I could not completely rid myself of my cultural conditioning. I drew the line at holding hands.

Insisting it was time for my departure, I stood across the room from mother and daughters, awkwardly reciting my gratitude and waving goodbye, as physical contact was not permitted. Everyone wore their new clothes in preparation for visiting their extended family and friends. They beseeched me to join them but I knew these visits would occupy many days. They explained with painstaking confusion that whatever a person does on No Ruz will affect the rest of the year. If a person is warm and kind to their relatives, friends and neighbours then the coming year will be a good one. I believed they felt genuine affection for me but also feared unkindness would bring bad luck. Zahra could not restrain herself and hugged my leg pleading with me not to leave, tears brewing in her eyes.

Flanked by a cavalcade of disorderly motorbikes and a tractor piled high with cheering youngsters we paraded through streets, horns blaring and engines revving. After hugs and kisses all around, I pedalled away looking back at the happy sight of thirty guys blocking the road and waving me off. I had escaped lightly with only one burnt arm and loudly ringing ears but with the memories of an eventful few hours.

10

Oh Lisdoonvarna

My moods were erratic and people's initial reaction to me depended largely on my state of mind at the time. Due to tiredness I often came across as being reserved or grumpy and subsequently received sullen, unenthusiastic though rarely hostile responses. I arrived in villages where every human being, whether they were digging a ditch, chatting with a neighbour, wrestling with a donkey or taking a crap behind a bush, would stop and stare at me with frank curiosity. This often made me irritable as I don't generally thrive in the limelight. I tried desperately to suppress my idiotic conditioning of 'rudeness' but occasionally I stared back, eyes wide open in exaggeration but not once did they recognize my displeasure. Listening to shouts of 'hey tourist' or 'ahh mister' could easily be misconstrued as mockery when all the innocent narrator really intended was an offer of friendship.

Saying this however, most of the time I felt confident and cheerful thus more approachable. At each stop I made new friends who crowded around. They looked down the road from where I'd come, in search of my companions and thought it extremely comical that I was alone. They wanted to know why I had come and because I was on a humble bicycle assumed I could not afford to travel by airplane, air-conditioned bus or rented car like other rich foreigners. Men pulled up alongside to shake my hand before politely waving and turning their motorbikes around. Tea was forced on me by eager men who debated the sanity of tourists and were insulted by my naive attempt to pay for food shopping. They thanked God for bringing me to their table and prayed for my future safety.

A group of kids swarmed me in Shahindej. They had the cheek and unreservedness that only self-reliant street kids do. They scoffed my dinner without hesitation and threw stones at a rabid looking dog. One pulled what seemed to be a live headless pigeon out of his pocket and exchanged it with another for five cigarettes. His matted hair protruded at comical angles and little dimples appeared when he smiled. The bird's wings were taped but as the exchange took place it popped its head out and made a desperate dash for freedom. It flapped about wildly in the dust while being used as an objectionable football. I refused to buy bangers from a cocky little fella wearing all black and proudly displaying fake gold chains. He cursed me and offered heroine instead.

An hour later I found myself sitting in a leather chair behind the counter of a pharmacy, handing out bottles of cough medicine to puzzled old men. Hussain's impressive moustache dominated his face and he looked far older than his nineteen years. His elder brother Reza was intelligent and articulate and wore small spectacles. Their father, the owner of the shop, was adamant that I stay with them for the night. He enquired about the distribution of penicillin in Ireland and was thrilled when I told him that it was controlled. He criticized his government's policy of dishing it out for every ailment imaginable, resulting in poor people becoming addicted. We closed up shop to the dismay of the cueing customers and I followed their car to an upmarket part of town.

Plush carpets ran from wall to wall in their vast living room and a small set of lounge chairs surrounded a decorative table in one corner. Their mother received me graciously and thankfully did not object to my intrusion on this special evening. From the adjoining kitchen Zahra and Maryam, her two daughters, greeted me warmly in perfect English. Finally, their plump uneducated cousin Arman, visiting from Tabriz, kissed me with flabby cheeks. He was a natural comic and put everyone at ease with his hilarious rendition of the English language. I did not take offence.

Oh Lisdoonvarna

We stretched out on the floor and I struggled to overcome the agonizing pain in my backside. My knees were incapable of bending sufficiently, leaving me clinging onto my legs with my weight shifted forward in order to remain upright. I regularly lost my grip and fell back nearly knocking a hole in the wall with my head. Because I had spent so much time in this for me unnatural position, combined with the hours spent on the saddle, it felt as if I had inserted shards of glass in my backside. I smiled politely, my mind reeling in agony. This position also made eating cumbersome. I would hold one knee while grasping at handfuls of rice which trailed across the carpet, onto my trouser leg and clung to my shirt before I inserted the few remaining morsels into my disappointed mouth.

They were obviously a very affluent family but did not flaunt their wealth through expensive ornaments or ostentatious architecture. What was evident was the money that had been spent on all four children's education. They possessed impeccable manners and enjoyed holding a cultured conversation.

Zahra was the elder and the more reserved of the sisters. She wore traditional loose flowing clothes like her mother, with whom she obviously had a close bond. Maryam had been a student in Tehran for the past three years and showed signs of cosmopolitan living. She wore a fashionable knee length figure hugging *manteau* over flared jeans which, although conservative by Irish standards, would have been deemed quite inappropriate in certain homes. She was a self assured young woman, comfortable with her individuality. She enjoyed the relative freedom she had, the capital being less conservative than other religious centres like Qom. She told me how female students in Tehran, who outnumber the males, enjoy pushing the boundaries of self expression with headscarves pushed as far back as possible to show off new haircuts and expensive make-up. Her brow creased as she talked about the Gasht Ershad, or Morality Police, who are responsible for monitoring what is appropriate for women to wear under the constitution. They patrol the streets catching women with 'bad hijab' – boots too high, tunics too short, wearing nail polish or hair improperly covered.

Curious Companions

Maryam's world, as with millions of others, was split into two contrasting lives. In private she had freedom of expression, to debate with friends over fashions, politics and relationships, wore what she liked and acted as she pleased. In public however, she quietly conformed for fear of the repercussions.

Her honesty and charisma were attractive but I suppressed the urge to flirt, although our eyes did meet continuously across the busy room. We chatted about Western influence over life in Tehran, which she considered equally positive and destructive, while her brothers fought over the controls of a video camera. She made a conscious effort to tighten her hijab and seem more appropriate on this religious occasion. She was attentive to her brothers without feeling obligated. Although the formal status of the house still existed there was obvious mutual respect and love in this family.

It had been yet another eventful day and I lay next to a snoring Arman on the living room floor and marvelled at the endless hospitality I was receiving from such kind and tolerant people. I wished those who had worried about my travelling through Muslim countries could have seen me then.

The next day was the 21st of March or in the Iranian calendar 1st day of the 1st month 1387. The family celebrated this New Year's morning with haft seen – an elaborately prepared festive table including seven specific items starting with the letter S. The items symbolically corresponded to seven creations and the holy immortals protecting them. The decorative plastic sheet was adorned first with a mirror at the head, a pot of flowers, shoots of a barley plant with notes of Rials on top, a paste like dessert, sugar sweets, nuts, apples, garlic, a berry I'd never heard of before, lit candles, dried fruit, a tray of small yellow biscuits, a glass of vinegar and a bowl with three blasé gold fish swimming about. In all it seemed quite a random mix of items and food stuffs and I nodded politely, ignoring Reza's educational lesson about what each item represented.

Their dad calmly fingered prayer beads, silently contemplating next to the stove. He observed me for some time, running over the words he wished to use before questioning the religious divisions in Ireland. Everyone studied me carefully as I explained that the problems that revolve around Northern Ireland stem from colonization and are all too often misinterpreted as religiously motivated.

He enquired about my religious views and I tried to explain, as piously as possible, about my own disillusion with automatically accepting the beliefs of where one is born. I stared into his solemn eyes and related how I had the utmost respect for people's choices and even felt jealous of those who find comfort in religion, but that as yet I have refused to fully accept any one code. He held a Koran to his lips as if shielding himself. Reza urged me to continue, so I clarified that in my opinion if a God does exist, no matter what title we mortals chose to give him, it will be a person's heart that will ultimately decide one's fate. Putting to good use one's talents and abilities and living life to the full, while being honest, kind and compassionate, is what I consider important. His father said he felt humbled, I felt like a preacher.

Korans, old and new, were passed around. In turn everyone kissed and touched their heads repeatedly on the holy book, before murmuring prayers in hushed whispers. Arman head butted the book and laughed as if pretending to faint. He turned up the volume on the TV and sang along with a pop song. Everyone bowed their heads to conceal their giggles, his uncle scratched his forehead and closed his eyes in concentration. The mother held her hands aloft and praised the Lord.

The exact moment of the arrival of spring was announced on TV. Everyone clapped, cheered and took turns kissing and embracing each other but of course I could only touch the men. I felt ridiculous waving my best wishes across the room, with a small bow for good measure, to the similarly embarrassed females. Arman grabbed my ass.

Their gracious mother blessed the whole proceedings with splashes of rose water. With blushing cheeks she then handed out the notes that had decorated the barley to everyone's competitive displays of gratitude. I had firstly been invited unreservedly into their home, fed copious amounts of delicious food, been entertained by their charm and intellect, been accepted into their private religious celebration and now they forced me to accept money as a token of their gratitude. We signed each other's notes as a keepsake and a mark of good luck.

Curious Companions

Zahra, to complete the episode of goodwill, gave me one of her caricature drawings which will remind me forever of this special occasion spent with these extraordinary people.

The day was already hot as I followed the valley with large peaks of stubborn rock jutting out above hillsides of dusty red clay. From the shade of a thorny bush I ate oranges and watched a man herd his sheep along a stream. The subsequent few hours were a battle of attrition against a steep gradient and strong winds.

I pulled up alongside a group of young men to ask directions and was once again welcomed with dramatic expressions of friendship. The most boisterous of the group was a sturdy young man with a large bushy ginger beard framing a bright smile. He was built like a *prop* and would have looked more at home driving a tractor at the ploughing championships in Thurles, than on a street corner in the mountains of central Iran. He grasped my shoulders with muscular hands and pulled me in close to plant three kisses on alternate cheeks. Feeling the wiry hair of his beard brush against my cheek reminded me of kissing my dad good night when I was a boy.

Having checked into a dull hotel, I sat on the roof with the receptionist, gazing at the red setting globe disappearing behind grey tiled rooftops. He dreamt of becoming an astronaut and his claim to have great eyesight, better than Europeans, was in his world reason enough to be sought after by Nasa. He yearned to use his 'extraordinary skill' to better the life of the planet. I didn't question his logic as indeed his eyesight was better than mine. He was worried about the women he might meet due to his impending fame. He had somehow been informed about their 'bad habits', no doubt referring to having multiple partners before marriage and living an independent lifestyle. 'Your women all suffer from the sickness of AIDs,' he worried.

I assured him no manic, AIDs-infected, sex-addicted women would kidnap him and force him to comply against his will to their evil ways. This he found reassuring so asked me for money to buy new underwear.

While eating dinner I chatted intermittently with an egotistic man from Tehran. He told me proudly how he was a quality control expert for a Swiss company specializing in metal piping. He sought my admiration but received my commiseration for having, what seemed to me, the most boring job on the planet. Like most men who were desperate to prove their wealth and portray their modern lifestyles, he sought to include his possessions in our conversation whenever possible. I was glad when he left to use his satellite cellphone to call his ambassador of an uncle in Canada about the importation of an important electrical device which was integral to the country's process of modernization. 'Excuse me I have to go wash my clothes in the river. I sincerely hope that works out for you,' I said insincerely.

Before sunrise at a small cupboard-sized shop, I bought dried fruit and nuts, scooping them from large sacks. The timid owner adjusted his droopy white prayer hat, looked into my eyes and stroked my hand, showing affection that surpassed any words. Plastic signs spoilt the beauty of decorated doorways and mud packed village walls. I toiled my way over an undulating landscape, reaching the hilltop only to float down and begin the process over again. I sheltered from the scorching sun under a single boulder, the only shade for twenty kilometres. A burnt out fire, rusting tin cans and syringes littered the sand. I found myself in the lair of local junkies.

Open backed trucks whizzed by. Women sat passively in the rear amongst wooden boxes and piles of firewood. Although I had been using copious amounts of atomic resistant suncream my skin was succumbing to the intense heat. Blisters formed on the backs of my hands and my neck was raw to the touch. Regrettably I donned my woolly winter gloves and hung boxer shorts from the rear of my cap for added protection.

I ate kebabs and was treated like an alien. I craved ice cream and was taken for a celebrity. I purchased a t-shirt and had to threaten the shopkeeper before he would accept my money. I bought food and was mercilessly taken for a fool. A kind hotel owner refused payment from his 'guest' and his sons tried to poison me with an 'apple' *hookah*.

One day in the sandy inhospitable countryside I was flanked by four guys on two motorbikes. It was an hourly occurrence in those uneventful parts as young men lounged about the roadside letting their youth drift by with as little effort as possible. After the obligatory questions our conversation fell flat, as it habitually did. They stared at me with impatient eyes, as if anticipating a magic trick or some type of performance. When I didn't indulge their need for entertainment they resorted to mockery. The comforting words of Christy Moore kept me company,

> 'Shur everybody needs a break
> Climb a mountain or jump in a lake.
> Some head off to exotic places,
> Others go to the Galway Races.
> Mattie goes to the South of France,
> Jim to the dogs, Peter to the dance.
> A cousin of mine goes potholing,
> A cousin of hers loves Joe Dolan.
> Summer comes around each year,
> We go there and they come here.
> Some jet off to... Frijiliana,
> But I always go to Lisdoonvarna.....
> Ohhhhh Lisdoonvarna....
> A lissdoon lissdoon lissdoonvarna.'

To rid myself of the undesirable attention I stopped for a break but when I resumed my smug antagonists were waiting, revving their bikes beside the body of a burnt out oil tanker. They were relishing our game of cat and mouse knowing full well their engines and numbers gave them an unfair advantage. They shouted obscenities, threw nuts at my head and swerved hoping I might crash. With a chocolate bar, I lured the most callous snorting ruffian towards me. As he grasped it from my hand I thrust my electric tazer gun into his leg.

'....Ohh Lissdoonvarna.
Motorbikes and Hi-ace vans,
With bottles - barrels - flagons - cans.
Mighty craic. Loads of frolics,
Pioneers and alcoholics,
PLAC, SPUC and the FCA,
Free Nicky Kelly and the IRA.
Hairy chests and milk-white thighs,
And mickey dodgers in disguise.'

In a market in Istanbul I had gone in search of this device which although legal in America is forbidden in Europe. It is about the size of an old mobile phone and enclosed in a plastic casing with two ominous metal pins protruding from the top. 30,000 volts surge through these pins into the unlucky recipient, inflicting incredible pain and causing partial loss of bodily functions. The impressive sound and blue lightning bolt alone would discourage an assailant thinking he was about to claim an easy victim, or so I had thought. Thus far I had only used it for scaring away dogs at night but today I had no empathy for my newly acquired entourage.

His face became an inspired theatrical performance of sudden contorted expressions. He dropped the chocolate to the passing tarmac. The tttutuzzz of escaping electric was clear over the hum of the engine. My foe fell sideways, pulling his driver off balance. Thankfully no cars were on the road as the pair zigzagged for quite a distance, desperately trying to regain control before diving head first into the dust. The bike continued along the road as if by remote control until it lost momentum and toppled over with a clatter of plastic fenders.

'Mc Graths, O'Briens, Pippins, Coxs,
Massage parlours in horse boxes.
There's amhráns, bodhráns, amadáns,
Arab sheiks, Hindu Sikhs, Jesus freaks,
RTE are makin' tapes, takin' breaks and throwin' shapes.
This is heaven, this is hell.
Who cares? Who can tell?
Anyone for the last few Choc Ices, now?
Ohhhhh Lisdoonvarna...'

Genius!

The possibility of retribution was on my mind as I continued towards Malayer but thankfully four cheerful guys on one motorbike joined me on the outskirts and swore to defend me with their lives. They wore their best figure-hugging shirts with black synthetic trousers and called, 'mister, mister,' incessantly asking questions. They guided me to several hotels, some full, others derelict. Eventually hidden down an alleyway we convinced a receptionist that I was not a threat and merely a lost tourist. I thanked my valiant guardians before encountering another five guys in vests posturing in the hall. One had 'Sexy' on his baseball cap and another 'Babe' on his pink t-shirt. I wondered who they were trying to impress. They scowled, presumably resenting my intrusion of their territory. I untucked my oily trousers from my socks and enquired if they had a problem, feeling confident with my weapon in my pocket. There was no problem, so I went for a shower until the water ran out leaving me with frothy shampoo in my hair. I wiped away the foam using the brown stained bed sheets and put my sweaty clothes back on. I ventured past reception in search of food and left behind a gaggle of laughter.

It was five a.m. when I mounted the following morning. I had begun rising early to avoid the day's worst heat. Before long though the sun became relentless, the road a shimmering haze. Families picnicked so I did likewise. I lay on grass with thistles and pine needles piercing my back. Two families rolled their cars to a halt, obscuring my view of a seemingly laughing corpse of a dog. The ground was littered with smashed glass, plastic bags caught on briars and oil cans clung to stained gravel. Blankets and pillows were spread on the driveway of a derelict bungalow, large containers of food and drinks were set out and a tent completed the arrangement. Three generations of the two families piled inside. It was to me a ludicrous scene as the interior, cut off from the breeze, must have been excruciatingly hot in the midday sun. Deafening lorries coughed out toxic fumes and shook the ground as they trundled past only metres away.

The first greeting sign I'd seen in English faced me as I left a town, 'Welcome to the city of flowerword and martyrdom and divine knowledge'. Martyrdom is something that towns are extremely proud of in the Islamic Republic. Pictures of the local dead who had sacrificed their lives fighting 'evil' were plastered onto sign boards and painted on concrete walls. I can understand the attraction of martyrdom, but I wonder how much is peer pressure on the impressionable, combined with a desperate desire to be remembered, a type of vanity after death.

The air was warm as the sun receded behind the horizon so I decided to sleep out. I wanted to escape the squalid hotels and feel closer to my surroundings. I wished to find a homely cave or abandoned hut but had to settle for a large drainpipe under the road as the desert doesn't provide much natural protection. It did seem somewhat desperate but it was in fact quite perfect. I swept away sand and stones and laid my sleeping bag out. The circumference of the pipe was about two metres and I blocked a breeze from one end with my bags. I ate dried fruit for dinner and lay reading my book by lamplight, feeling cosy and protected from the elements. I was unconcerned by stories of wild beasts and kidnappings. The latter I had been warned about continuously but figured if it were going to happen there was just as much chance it would during the day as at night. I felt invisible curled up in my tunnel.

The chilly morning air woke me, the large orb of the moon hovered over sharp mountaintops. Oases of pink and purple flowering apple trees dotted pale green fields. Not long into the day I suffered an infuriating list of bike problems which left me in a temper tantrum. I sweated profusely, flung the pump at a bush and kicked a tree in disgust. I sat on the ground and held my throbbing foot. Tiredness and irritation had set in after so many repetitive days.

Although my bike was giving me problems it seemed as if the whole community was keen to help. The driver of a pickup truck offered me a lift so I jumped in the back with a butchered wheel and a blistered tube. He looked back at me repeatedly, waving with one hand while cradling his daughter in the other. At a petrol station the

Curious Companions

greasy attendants fixed the problems with ease and invited me to their home. Their overalls were too short and they yanked at their crotches in tandem. Regrettably I had to push on so got a lift from two guys on a motorbike back to my abandoned bike.

My tribulations amended, I sat with several men eating apples and watched a group of city tourists pose for photos on an old Massy Ferguson tractor. These wise old men were completely content to sit in silence and enjoy each other's company. There was no need for conversation, no small talk or chit chat, just the rare bursting statement one may feel the impulsive need to get off one's chest. They were happily bored without a trace of irritation. No need for entertainment as us Europeans demand every second of the day. I wished I could keep my indisciplined mind as still as theirs seemed to be. I gave one a departing gift of my red woolly hat.

That evening a teenage boy herded goats amongst rocks on the slopes of a mountain pass. I waved out to him as he approached with hesitation and we shared what little food I had left. His poverty was obvious from his scrawny body and tattered clothes. Dirt beads clung to his neck. A desperate look of hunger and loneliness subdued his youthful demeanour. We spent an enjoyable evening together in his rickety wooden shed along with two playful new born kids with silky smooth floppy ears.

He was attentive to his dog which was likewise malnourished, with bloodshot eyes, a patchy coat and only one ear. She licked my hand but feeling unfulfilled returned to her private parts. We threw stones at piled up rocks and cheered when they collapsed. He watched wide eyed as I showed him a movie clip of cycling through London on my camera. He was oblivious to the wonders and horrors of the modern world. His flock bleated in the silent night air.

At dawn he sipped his portion of warm milk with careful relish. I moaned as I put on my wet shoes. He had only decayed sandals. He smiled and poured milk into my water bottle. He was ignorant of self pity, a virtue I wish I possessed. I felt foolish and unworthy of his kindness. I continued down the road feeling guilty for having been blessed with such a privileged life.

11

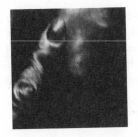

Dazzling Domes
and Damsels in Distress

An injury to my ankle manifested itself out of the bleak mountainscape. Sweat dripped from my furrowed brow as I agonized with each turning pedal. I was guessing my Achilles tendon had been damaged and I pushed down with one leg, holding the other dangling by my side. I had hoped to reach Esfahan but stopped at a hotel thirty kilometres short of the city. I crawled up the steps and hopped on one leg to the reception. With every movement I could feel the muscle tearing.

'Greetings of course my good friend,' said the esoteric receptionist.

'Hello, can I have a room please?' I replied, not in the most sociable of moods.

'Of course sir, you are the mostest special welcomer we have in our hotel there.'

'That's fantastic. How much is it?'

'Of course, for you most bravest cyclist we have nice small room for all your friends. Is nice price with big view from upper hotel.' His smile was as fake as if he had been politely waiting a month for a photo to be taken.

'Ok well yes all I need is a small room. I am travelling alone. And please could you give me one on the ground or first floor?'

'Of course, the ground is good in Iran, big bed with good view of country.' His head was heavy and drooped. He pushed thick glasses back as they slid down his nose and squinted with magnified eyes.

'Can you please show me a room on the ground floor? Thank you.' I hopped off and beckoned him to follow. I found an adequate empty room and lay down telling my host that I would not be moving no matter how good the view was. I paid him to pay a guy who ordered his son to carry my things inside. 'Good night and God bless,' I chimed while closing the door.

He seemed perplexed.

The pre-dawn traffic consisted of lorries seemingly on fire with black smoke billowing out from underneath. My nostrils stung with every breath as I patiently rolled my way into Esfahan. The boulevards were lined with green trees. Immaculately dressed policemen directed me with surprising efficiency.

I installed myself in a popular yet foul tourist hostel, smeared cold gel on my ankle, wrapped it in ice, took anti-inflammatory tablets and indulged in two days of non-existence. An obnoxiously nice guy from Tehran who cared for the plight of flamingos bought me an ice cream. A group of Swedish feminists, tired of seeing women depicted as sexual objects in Europe, now detested the fact they could not display their bodies. I urged them to fight for their rights and encouraged them to get naked. They said I was sexist.

The following day I ventured out to Imam Reza Square with a young English fellow of Sri Lankan decent and a local in his sixties who worked part-time at the guesthouse. Simon claimed in a rather posh London accent that he liked to surround himself with intelligent people. I laughed at Akbar who thought a fly had entered his ear hole. Picnicking families enjoyed the atmosphere of the second largest square in the world. Couples circled in horse drawn carriages, reminding me of Killarney. Repetitive archways hid a bazaar and high above grand tiled domes and minarets dominated the skyline.

We lay on the grass as Akbar licked his lips and told us of a Dutch girl who he had taken on a tour of an ancient castle located in the mountains some years before. His tongue escaped his mouth as he

126   *Curious Companions*

demonstrated how he had kissed her passionately while they had watched a camel.

'She like me very much this girl. She like camel too. She like kiss me very much this girl too.'

Simon's expression was utter revulsion.

'I show her nice things and my things too.' He sniggered and raised an eyebrow for effect.

'But is that not illegal?' Worried Simon.

'No no sir. It is good thing to show woman tourist nice things. Bad for man tourist to show Iran woman nice things. Muslim woman not like see things because she not like. Is forbidden by our most gracious God Allah, Peace be upon Him'.

Akbar was leaning in close to the Englishman who reclined, terrified the tongue would reappear.

'Yahhh we had good time too. But police come. Everything ok. They let me go with only small money pay and send Kat to her country. Maybe I go to Dutch and kiss Kat more.' He looked towards the sky dreamily.

I rolled about laughing. Simon doubted the validity of the story and interrogated Akbar about the deportation process. Akbar thumped himself on the side of the head and said, 'Fly in my ear, fly in my ear.'

I left the two lads in hot debate about the moralities of cross-cultural relationships and went to explore the Imam Mosque. Amazingly complex designs in turquoise, dark blues and golds flowed up the walls culminating in domes high above. I twirled around gazing up at the mosaics for a long time and nearly fell over with dizziness when a sweet female voice appeared by my side. Standing only two feet away was a beautiful young woman with white silk headscarf floating on a stylish hairdo. Next to her was a man whom I cared little about. She introduced herself as an English teacher from Tehran who was visiting Esfahan with her family. Her dad shook my hand as I stared at his daughter unsure what to say. He was obviously there as chaperone and I was glad she also ignored him. I forgot her name but it was already too late to ask again. Her face had delicate features with subtle makeup and long alluring eyelashes. She was dressed in a contour defining shirt and stood with one arm resting gently on a hip. She looked phenomenal.

We talked freely about the basics of our lives and joked when a crowd congregated to watch us chat. She claimed to like theatre but I thought she was a terrible actress. She began to lose her confidence in front of so many inquisitive eyes. I was shaking. Her dad didn't seem to mind that we flirted freely and shoed away some of the more unruly onlookers. People shouted out questions for her to ask me and she patiently did so, all the while apologizing for the awkward situation. I craved to pick her up and whisk her away but instead squirmed at the inevitable question about my religious beliefs asked by a sullen old man.

She spoke in perfect English but I remember little of what she said. She had a broad smile and vivacious personality. Her beauty was captivating and yet again I found myself incredibly attracted to a girl I had only just met. I was dazed by her brazen approach with the support of her father. He now stood recording the scene by video phone, coming up close to record our blushing faces and panning out around the accumulated crowd. Having exchanged addresses I stood and watched her stride across the courtyard and disappear out of sight. The crowd looked at me and I suppressed the urge to run after her. Simon and Akbar showed up a few minutes later and told me excitedly about a gorgeous girl they had just seen. Akbar said she was famous and that he had killed the fly. I felt happy for him.

The city took obvious pride in its appearance with lush parks and flower beds surrounding the Zayandeh River. Huge trees overhung the usual traffic and seemed to calm the chaos. Decorative bridges spanned the river and people posed for photos. Groups of guys checked out groups of girls who giggled and shielded themselves with their hijabs.

Farhad, Akbar's son, took me by the hand through a bazaar where people haggled over goods. Down a small hidden alleyway we ducked low through a tunnel decorated in hanging lamps and entered a smoky cauldron of a tea room. I was relieved when I got my hand back. The walls and ceiling were covered with lanterns and lampshades of every possible description. We sat at a miniature table opposite a scowling

Curious Companions

man with a scar splitting his lips in four. A group of bearded men dominated the atmosphere with arguments and the waiter with continuous demands. I looked away sheepishly as they gesticulated something in my direction. Two lean brothers with wispy grey hair protruding from their hats, suckled on hookahs engulfing themselves in a cloud of mint smoke. Eighties hippy style orange globes nestled next to Japanese painted glass flutes and the lower walls were decorated with dark armoury. Above my head were photos of the owner standing sour faced beside various famous individuals. That very man sat behind a wooden counter gathering and handing out wads of notes with one hand, puffing fervently on his pipe with the other. Farhad swore the owner had not left his hidden cavern or stopped smoking since its establishment thirty five years previously. He was averse to talking and would not smile for anyone. We sipped tea from china saucers and added our contribution to the haze.

Farhad had a sudden carnivorous craving so we went next door where we plucked a sheep's heart out of a bucket of blood. The heart was chopped into small chunks with blood squirting out over the wooden counter and then fondled onto metal skewers. It is considered a grave insult to refuse food in Iran. I didn't baulk at the idea of what I was about to eat but worried about the health consequences. The tough and rubbery meat didn't taste bad but I swallowed with regret. Farhad was sombre faced and related his love for his cousin who had chosen to marry another relative over him. I found this common tradition of marrying first cousins difficult to get used to. The strands of bloody organ stuck between my teeth weren't particularly pleasing either.

That evening I found myself lost in a quiet alleyway lined by tall mud walls when I felt my stomach lurch and expel its uninvited contents. I spent an hour crouched behind a van in distress. Dogs came to investigate the noises of anguish. I apologized as they fled from the hideous sight.

The morning after, I sat sulking in the corner of the hostel courtyard minding my own business, when a young Korean girl in distress sat down opposite me. I peered at the numerous empty tables surrounding us and contemplated moving. Mimi ripped off her head scarf and slapped it indignantly on the wobbly plastic table, spilling my coffee.

'Do you speak English, hello?' She huffed.

'Yes I do.'

'Could you tell these idiots I'm not paying their stupid room rates? They try over charge me you know. Just because I am a woman they think I am stupid.' I was tempted to concur with them.

'What rates did they ask you for?'

'40,000 Rials (3 Euro) for one room only. They are bad man.' She struggled out of her black shirt, head tilted back, extending neck muscles. She stroked her liquorish black hair, pumped out her breasts and stretched.

'They charged me double that. Would you like to share my room?' I offered.

She adjusted the side of her bra. 'You are lucky. You are a man. You can do what you like. All Iran man are perverts.' She squashed her breasts together with both hands as if trying to compress them.

I swallowed hard and dribbled coffee on my only clean t-shirt. The cleaning lady glared at her from an open window. The male receptionist approached and asked her apologetically to put her clothes and hijab back on while in the common area.

'I hate this country,' she said as the man walked away.

After some coffee Mimi calmed down. I negotiated a room for her at nearly a third the rate I was paying. She seemed pleased with herself. She told me about her life since she entered Iran two weeks before. Arriving in Tabriz from Turkey by bus, she had been accosted by a lone man who groped her. She fought him off with slaps and screams as he grabbed her ass and tried to kiss the lone innocent female. On her second day she ventured out nervously in search of food and once again found she was being followed. Her new admirer walked past grinning and around the next corner confronted her, his cotton trousers around his ankles, his penis in his hand and a large smile on his face. She didn't know where to look as the guy masturbated frantically in the quiet street. She retreated but the man shuffled after her, his trousers dragging in the dust. She ran straight to the police station where she cried but

Curious Companions

the police refused to let her file a report. She boarded a bus to Tehran and went straight to the Korean Embassy where she was provided with free accommodation and a police escort. This she found laughable.

I felt bad for her having had such unpleasant experiences in a country where the vast majority of people had treated me with the utmost respect. I felt people did not deserve the reputation she was casting over them and thought it my duty to show her what kind, hospitable people the majority of Iranians really are.

It was the thirteenth day of the No Ruz festival, named Sizdah Bedar, literally 'thirteen to out' or figuratively speaking - hit the outdoors on the thirteenth. It is a much anticipated day where families picnic in the countryside. We walked along the city's deserted streets watching traffic lights flicker and asked a forgotten old man for directions.

The crowded park had a jovial atmosphere with lazy city dwellers lying about on blankets, watching their young fight and their old sleep. We unpacked our miserable picnic of nuts, chocolate and unidentifiable fruits. A man whizzed past on roller blades, frightening a flock of cloaked women. People approached to take photos of us with their mobile phones. Some secretive, some brazen. Children rolled up their trousers and waded in the murky waters of a pond. Families called out to us to join them from all around but we declined politely. I had predicted this would happen and even though Mimi was apprehensive I eventually gave in to a persistent man with an enormous nose who pulled on my arm.

The men greeted me with firm handshakes and the womenfolk nodded shyly. I tried desperately to avoid questions about being husband and wife. I knew it was unacceptable for two unrelated young people of the opposite sex to be alone together, so eventually conceded that we had indeed been married the previous year. This was received with great applause. Mimi pulled her headscarf half covering her face in mortification and eyed me none too happily. Round after round of delicious food was piled onto our plates and at one point three glasses of various soft drinks awaited my attention.

No Ruz lasts twelve days. The thirteenth day is spent avoiding the bad luck associated with the number thirteen by going outdoors away from possible mishaps. At the end of the celebrations the sabzeh, or barley plant grown for the haft deen, which has symbolically collected all sickness and bad luck, is thrown into running water to exorcise the demons from the household.

Mimi was given the honour. The family all gathered by the river's edge holding hands and congratulating one another. Many other groups eager to watch the foreigners swarmed around and waved whenever I looked up. Mimi held the bunch of grass as if it were about to explode and tossed it into the brown current. She turned around grinning ecstatically, delighted to have been accepted at last. Grim faces in the crowd lowered their gaze. Her head scarf had tragically fallen unnoticed to her shoulders. Not a good sign for the coming years luck.

The desert stretched to the horizon. Scraggy bushes were the only evidence of life and tumble weed blew in the wind. Whirlwinds picked up dust and rubbish and carried it away. I stopped for my obligatory chelo kebab which I had been eating almost every day from lack of choice. A skewered piece of meat was served on a mound of rice with raw onion on the side and sections of enormous flat bread were used as a shovel. It was a decent and filling meal but eaten two or even three times a day became somewhat bland. Occasionally 'restaurants', which were no more than three walled rooms with a scattering of chairs, a table and a gas cooker in the corner, had bowls of vegetables or beans in watery sauce or chicken pieces instead of lamb but these were rare.

At a bus shelter I met Abul Fadhl, a young guy who had a reputation for inviting foreigners to his home. He was suspicious and interviewed me about my exact characteristics.

'Do you have a good personality?' He began.

Curious Companions

'I don't know. I guess you will have to be the judge of that,' I said, already regretting my enquiry about staying with him.

'I don't let not good people stay with me.' He looked at his brother for confirmation but he looked away.

'Don't worry I will stay here tonight. It's nice and warm and I would like to spend the evening writing anyway. Thank you and nice to meet you.' I habitually chanced upon genuinely kind people who enjoyed helping others and disliked him for wanting me to plead for assistance. I did not want to stay with someone who demanded admiration for his goodwill.

'No no my friend I am a kind man. I will permit you to sleep in my house for free. People in this country spit on tourists. I help so many tourists. You will ask people and they will know Abul Fadhl. Now come we will go.'

His scowling brother held my eye and agreed with me that I should remain in the fly-ridden bus station but his younger brother was the boss of this operation.

I conceded and deposited my dusty bags in their spare room. The house had a pretty courtyard. His brother's wife sat behind a huge carpet loom fingering lines of cotton with dexterous fingers. She worked so fast I was convinced she would make a fantastic guitar player. Unfortunately there was still tension and I stared up at the fractures in the ceiling. Earthquakes had weakened the brickwork, Abul lamented.

His brother, I was shocked to hear, was a school teacher. He had a scary face and was a wonderful father. He played with his two young children with the loving affection of a devoted parent. Abul's father arrived and greeted me with a bear hug and a booming voice. 'Hello, hello. Goodbye, goodbye,' amplified as if through a loudspeaker.

Later on we ventured out to a shop where Abul enjoyed the attention we received. I was expected to perform like a monkey but was tired of the circus. My supervisor talked on his phone seemingly to anyone that would listen. I ate stale crisps, dreamed of the Monster Munch of old and tried to ignore the camp shop attendant who wore tight white jeans and a modified pink tank top revealing thin shaven arms. He sat with his legs tightly crossed, ignored customers, smoked a cigarette with a loose wrist and winked at me. I told Abul I would wait outside and sat on an old oil barrel listening to the wind whistle through electric pylons. A dog peed on a pole which held up a multi-coloured disco ball that squeaked as it slowly rotated. I was at the centre of the local disco scene. The shopkeeper leaned on the doorframe while feeling his own ass, patiently awaiting the arrival of the Gay Tour of Iran.

We left to investigate some ancient cooling towers which caught the day's winds, directing them deep into the ground to cool the water below. This was where at the age of eight Abul had met a sleeping German man, thus beginning his obsession with the eccentricities of the tourist.

Saying goodbye before sunrise I felt genuinely grateful to Abul. I agreed to his request to send a letter to Lonely Planet recommending the great Abul Fadhl as an unmissable attraction of Iran. Of course I had absolutely no intention of doing it. The last thing I wanted was to boost his over-inflated ego further. I can often be notoriously harsh on my benefactors. I blame the relentless hospitality of Iranians.

I turned up the tunes of *Paul Van Dyke* trying to distract myself from the simmering heat. It was a desolate landscape and I only passed one garage and one dilapidated compound over the course of two hours. The shade of a signpost provided the solitary slim shadow for miles around. I slept for three hours. Crows paused to see if I was still alive, human beings did not.

The wind swirled around, propelling me up to forty kilometres one second only to leave me seemingly reversing the next. I staggered into a shed adorned with a disintegrating Zam Zam sign and ordered four bottles of the revolting glowing orange concoction. Each contained at least twelve million cubes of sugar and tasted like feet.

The turquoise dome of a mosque lured me into its courtyard. The air was tranquil. Two men chatted in one corner and saluted me as I entered. I sat undisturbed as light streamed in through stained glass. A man entered and began his prayers. He stood with back straight, stomach protruding. He muttered Arabic and blinked. He placed the flats of his hands next to his ears. He bent forward a little uneasily. He

Curious Companions

straightened up again. He knelt cautiously. His hands and forehead gently touched the carpet. He sat up abruptly. He fell forward as if in search of mercy. It was time to stand. He muttered, signifying the start of the exercise once again. It was a routine beneficial for mind, body and soul.

I thought about the trip thus far. I had experienced a lot in a short amount of time but felt unsatisfied. Had I delved into people lives, learned from their experiences and enriched my own thoughts and values? Had I succeeded in ridding myself of my preconceptions and prejudices? Had I connected with people on an equal level, dealt with them as individual human beings and not as part of a stereotyped group?

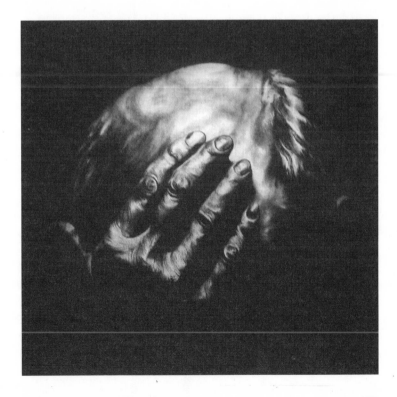

A soft murmur woke me from my slumber. The guardian of the mosque led me to an adjacent building where he served two plates of steaming rice topped with bean stew. I had become quite adept at cupping my fingers into a makeshift spoon and sat imagining the outrage had my grandmother seen my newly acquired table manners. A faded picture of Khomeini hung crooked from a wooden beam. His face dour yet confident, as if brooding over an injustice. My host was disinterested in talk and sat caressing his forehead with a calloused hand. We remained in silence, the only noises, the scribbling of my pen and the occasional rustling pages of his Koran.

I arrived at the stylish Silk Road Hotel in Yazd where independent backpackers and tour groups congregated to enjoy the modified Eastern experience. While I was eating my camel stew, Mimi arrived looking suitably flushed and irritated. It was nice to see a familiar face even if some of her perceptions seemed rather intolerant and racist to me.

We strolled around tiny alleyways, jumped down steps, ducked low under arches and posed for photos with foolish faces and fingers held up in peace signs. Down a narrow tunnel Mimi ripped off her headscarf and screamed, 'I want to get naked.' I was caught between sexual frustration and respect and I did not like it. There was obvious sexual tension between us as teasing me had become her most enjoyable pastime. She joked about my sexual deprivation and told me how a lot of younger Iranian women wear nothing under their burqas but sexy lingerie. She slowly licked an ice cream, her eyes never leaving mine.

Rejoining the swarm of shoppers in a bazaar I reminded Mimi to secure her head scarf which she had discarded into a pocket, not for my modesty but to prevent insulting the local women. She huffed and blamed me for her headache.

We sat in the courtyard of a mosque to escape the inquisitive crowds. Brittle old men washed their feet in the central pond, the reflection of the slender minarets contorted in the water. It was not merely a place of worship but a social area where people came to chat, study and relax. The old *madrasa* section was dilapidated. We lay on the dusty floor flicking through religious journals as light poured through lattice windows. I could imagine young boys lining the walls deep in concentration, learning by heart the words of Allah, enriching their thoughts, squandering their childhoods.

Climbing over the crumbling walls of a deserted castle we jumped from roof to roof of mud caked buildings, dodging washing lines and small chimneys. We circled up the stairs of a watch tower and peered out over the buzzing streets below. The call to prayer echoed around the city and twinkling domes and minarets silhouetted against the orange sky. We flirted, held hands and kissed.

A few seconds later back at the hotel we lay on Mimi's bed ravished with desire and excitement. I enjoyed watching her arching back, her taught snowy white neck and the roundness of her hips. She delighted in at last discarding her clothes as I rummaged frantically through my bags in search of condoms. Arnica cream, inhalers, puncture repair kits, antibiotics, soap, scissors, panadol and suncream were all there. Condoms, however, had taken leave.

Frustration is a horrible thing especially when it is given false hope. We went in the vain search of contraceptives. We lay on the bed some more. Mimi claimed to be on the pill but I was suspicious. We snuggled. I was screaming inside.

12

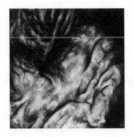

Deadly Desert

After a sleepless night I boarded a mini-van accompanied by two Swedes. We piled the bus high with plants from a garden centre and continued towards Kharanaq, an oasis village located in the barren desert mountains fifty kilometres north of Yazd.

The old town was dilapidated and deserted. Families now lived in new concrete boxes adjacent to the ancient settlement. We clambered up fragile staircases and ducked low through a labyrinth of connecting rooms and corridors. Crumbling walls were adorned with little windows that looked out across a patchwork of small irrigated fields. We tiptoed carefully over precarious rooftops and slipped through a broken window into the abandoned mosque. Pages of religious text were scattered over the carpet, metal pots gathered dust on a blue plastic table and graffiti covered white peeling walls. The Swedes were recording a video documentary of their trip and were continuously doing second or third takes of what they considered to be memorable shots. I found them crouched low in a corner zooming in on a spider while Jonas commentated on this supposedly deadly beast. The hamam next door had fallen victim to vandals. I tried to imagine the village men reclining in baths of steaming hot water talking about their crops or the Koran as Stefan posed for a photo pretending to take a crap.

An arched bridge spanned a dry riverbed and a path led to a half built mosque beyond. We scrambled up the loose rocky hillside to view the earthen coloured town lit up by a break in the clouds and backed by the dramatic dark rock of the mountain. Grey sand-dunes ran in the opposite direction and were an ominous, unforgiving sight. As we descended a camel came running down the river bed shuffling its feet, followed by its calf and two men freewheeling on a scooter. Jonas took off in pursuit and spent an hour filming the clumsy creature drinking from a pond. He imitated David Attenborough and convinced the men that he was filming for Swedish Al Jezeera. Stefan asked the owner wishfully if his animal was packed with opium. I too had heard rumours of camels trained to run for hundreds of kilometres across borders unaccompanied, drugs inserted under their skin. A unique way of drug smuggling seeing the authorities could not stop every wild camel from wandering the deserts between Afghanistan and Iran.

I felt a little apprehensive about the ever increasing heat and the rumours about kidnappings in the east of the country. An Irish cyclist had been kidnapped and held for one month along with two Germans while cycling near the Pakistani border in 2003. The convicted felons were later publicly executed. One Japanese backpacker had been taken from his hotel room in Bam six months ago and was still missing. The same group had also previously seized two Belgians. They demanded the release of their kin from prison or the return of large quantities of commandeered opium. I had also heard rumours about a group of Italians who had been attacked and two shot dead before the others were released but this was never confirmed. Some tourists had even been given police escorts while travelling on public buses for fear of another international incident. On the Department of Foreign Affairs website it was recommended that people avoid this part of Iran unless absolute necessary or postpone their trips if possible. I agonized over whether to risk continuing alone into the deserts of Baluchistan. I had come so far and was not afraid but knew my parents would not forgive me for taking such a gamble for the sake of accomplishment. Risking one's life is easy, knowing when to stop is the difficult part.

Curious Companions

The days became monotonous, uninspiring, empty desert. Many people believe deserts are awe-inspiring in their simplicity, I found them boring. Desolation overcame me. Lorrries irritated me. Telephone poles were my only companions. The voice of *Shane McGowen* catapulted me into the past, dancing drunkenly around an Irish Bar in Torremolinos to the words, 'Come all you rambling boys of pleasure, And ladies of easy leisure, We must say Adiós! Until we see, Almeria once again....'

One night in an under-road tunnel I was going through my routine of laying out my gear for the night when out jumped a man in military uniform with a white and black scarf around his neck. We stared at each other equally surprised before he called for backup. I was unsure if he was an official or a renegade. I had chosen a large tunnel that night as I had thought it would provide greater shelter from the wind. From both ends men jumped down into the sand as if it was a surprise raid. All except one wore combat outfits, one had a machine gun over his shoulder and another had a pistol drawn.

'Salaam Aleykum,' I said, offering biscuits.

They were thankfully army and were touchingly concerned for my safety. They reiterated the opinions of other officials that I should abandon cycling and take a bus. One man warned of blood thirsty robbers who would appear out of the night, armed with knives and slit my throat. His hand swiped at his windpipe, his head lolled to the side with a spluttering, choking sound. Everybody chuckled.

They invited me to stay at their barracks but I was unpacked, tired and quite liked sleeping out, so I declined. They were a fun bunch of misfits who chased each other and threw sand like children on a day trip to the seaside. I felt safer under my own protection. I studied the delicate snake trails in the sand and fell into a deep sleep.

It was dark when I awoke. Sand fell on my face and the wind howled. I spat grit out of my mouth and wiped a layer off my face. I tried to open my eyes but was blinded by the sand in the air. I built my bags up to protect my head but the wind was fierce and ignored my makeshift defence. I hid under my sleeping bag but the heat was so intense I strained to inhale, choking on sand.

As I groped around in the fresh sand-dune for my torch and inhaler, the barking began. I felt blind and lost. My asthma had deteriorated quickly and I fought to breathe. The barking intensified. A pack of dogs had somehow located me in the night and rightly predicted that I would be an easier target during the storm. Angry wailing cries came from both sides of the tunnel. Thankfully my fumbling hand caught hold of my torch and next to it I uncovered my shock gun. I was at least armed now but still felt defenceless being unable to open my eyes because of the sand thrashing my face.

During an ebb in the storm the growling grew frantic. A dog darted towards me, angry and invisible. I swung the pump about wildly and engaged the electric bolt from the gun which thankfully deterred the creature. It snarled and backed off uncertain. Another arrived a minute later but luckily I caught it on the head with a large rock and it yelped off. I used my bike as a barrier and flung stones into the darkness until the attack abated. I lay still for several hours listening intently to the dejected pack whimper and yap hungrily nearby. I longed to have a real gun to put the sordid creatures out of their misery.

The world was still and silent as the morning slowly matured. I dug my belongings out of the sand-dune that had built up around me. I shook sand from my bags, clothes and hair, wiped a layer from my skin and dug some out of my nose and ears. To my utter surprise rain began to fall. Large droplets struck the scorched land. I looked around at the flat endless desert and enjoyed the respite from the intense heat.

In Kerman, I splashed through large dirty puddles and evaded several police checkpoints. They regularly lined the road mostly searching suspicious vehicles for smuggled goods or people. They consistently asked the same questions and were unsure about how to deal with me. I wished them farewell after a couple of minutes, ignoring their requests to wait until they could get confirmation from a superior officer. I had refused to stop several times knowing the senseless routine. While leaving the city however, I was summoned to halt by a whistling military man brandishing a machine gun. He had sweaty rolls of fat around his neck. I was dragged off the bike, interrogated and bundled into an open backed truck. It had been decided by an invisible authority that I would no longer enjoy my freedom and would take the bus to Zahedan.

People gathered to see who was being guarded by armed sentries. I sat on the ground dejected, awaiting the departure of my bus. I had entered Baluchistan where men wore rough turbans and had skin as tough as elephant hide. Several tried to talk to me but were harassed and driven away by the bullying security guards. The majority of the crowd were heavily under the influence of what I presumed was opium. They babbled and swayed on their feet. Their clothes were torn and they seemed to care little about themselves or the guards who threatened them.

It is common knowledge that South Eastern Iran is awash with cheap drugs pouring into the country from Afghanistan. The local population is accused of assisting in the transportation of seventy percent of Europe's heroine through their lands. I had expected to see some down and outs in back alleyways but I was shocked to see the problem so evident around me.

I resentfully boarded the bus, looking down at a crowd of sour depleted faces. I was incensed at having to end my continuous three months of cycling but was left with little choice. I looked out at the desert flashing by and felt a deep regret. I was detached and defeated. I was being transported by the fumes of a noisy machine.

An extremely hairy man sitting opposite looked at me blankly with bloodshot eyes and wiped drool from his bushy mouth with a dirty sleeve. He was almost paralyzed under the influence of drugs. His eyes were bulging from their sockets and was unable to close his gaping mouth. His every movement was as if in slow motion. Raising hands to his face he stared intensely at dirty fingers. With little control over his body he lurched around his seat with the movement of the bus. I thought about stories I'd heard of drug addicted parents selling their children to support their habits. The majority of men and young boys sucked on lumps of putty like paste which was put into a small section of ripped napkin and then placed under the lower lip. It contained a mixture of tobacco, some unknown plant and a powdered rock and was apparently both very addictive and extremely detrimental to one's health.

The bus stopped not long into our journey for evening prayer. Men took up their positions in a ring of stones, their heads bowed in preparation for submission. I opened the underneath compartment of the bus and dragged my bike from under a pile of plastic bags and cotton bundles. I watched my seatmate stagger, making circles in the earth, unsure of where he was. He collapsed in the dust, closed his eyes and went to sleep with a final grunt. I felt both contempt and sympathy for him as I didn't know what had driven him to such depths.

It felt good to propel myself along the dark road, feeling the warm night air brushing against my face. Car lights illuminated the world at infrequent intervals. People believed it was too dangerous to drive at night. A gentle old man served me rice and a watery soup tasting of soap. I lay down on a bench at the back of his tea shop and slept soundly listening to the hum of his prayers.

Bam, a fertile desert oasis is a city under construction. The once prosperous agricultural and trading centre was home to two hundred thousand people before an earthquake flattened it in 2003. Seventy percent of the city was destroyed as fragile mud brick homes capsized, suffocating people as they slept.

I cycled around streets lined with date palms and mountains of rubble. Temporary dwelling units looked peculiar amongst the debris and ugly new construction was slowly taking place. A sense of quiet grief had replaced the initial despair. The thriving tourism industry had vanished and although I was welcomed with open arms, I knew foreigners would never again return in the same numbers.

At a stale new hotel I talked to the clean shaven owner about how just four days before the Bam earthquake, another earthquake measuring the same 6.5 on the Richter scale had shaken the state of California. The story was distressing as in America only three had died, as compared to over forty thousand in his beloved city. A truly shocking difference contrasting the effective modern building methods of the West with the traditional approach of the East. He asked why his people had been punished by the 'Will of God'. He explained in a quivering voice how the people of Bam had been told by the country's leading mullahs that it was a 'divine test' and to 'raise your hands to God and pray'. He munched on a date and thanked me for the help of international aid agencies who came with practical support both during and after the devastating event.

I was now on the outskirts of the vast Dasht-é-Lût desert and just three hundred and fifty kilometres west of the Pakistan border. The sky was clear and the road smooth. I was ready for a stretch of desert to last two days without interruption by civilization. 'Much danger for tourist on bicycle,' said the friendly officer.

I had been stopped once again and was being entertained with tea and cakes.

'Yes I am aware there are some bad people,' I responded, 'but I think they have no business with a poor Irish man.'

'Snakes live in sand and also ride camels.'

I guessed he was referring to the Baluchi tribes, a minority group who, along with the Kurds, have endured many years of hardship and constitute one of the poorest and least developed communities in Iran. The authorities are able to mask many of the measures they take against Baluchi political activists by claiming that they are cracking down on bands of smugglers and drug-traffickers. Baluchis have been moved to remote desert areas while outsiders have been encouraged to move in to take their place in towns, by providing incentives like free land, subsidized housing and government jobs.

'Thank you for the tea and may God keep your house safe.' I strode out into the blinding sunshine. Everyone followed.

I was wrong to expect the hardened yet polite officer to take orders from a young scruffy looking infidel and found myself once again being driven to the bus station. I had been courteously hijacked.

Together with drug trafficking, the presence of more than a million refugees from the continuing war in Afghanistan and the ready availability of arms through Pakistan, have contributed to instability in the region. Clashes between the security forces and the local population are common and this man would not take a chance with my life even if I would have. The bus driver was ordered to keep a close eye on me and only dispense with me in Zahedan. The officer took my hand in his and said that my wellbeing was in his heart. I watched out the back window as he waved me off.

The bus driver escorted me to a grubby hotel and had a long animated discussion with the receptionist before I was led to a room where the bed looked as if a camel had sat on it, crushed two wooden

Curious Companions

legs and wiped its ass on the torn sheet. I washed my dust caked body with a bucket of fantastically cold water.

Down at the 'dining hall', I wrote and swatted ravenous mosquitoes. A small man with beady eyes sucked on tobacco and told me his life story. He was a Kurd visiting Baluchistan on business. He dealt with import and export and claimed his brother had big connections in Tehran. He was proud that he took advantage of the corruption in government. He claimed to deserve the good life that he was living as compensation for his people's suffering. He often travelled to Turkey and Thailand on business trips that were a disguise for sex holidays. I chewed on rice and ignored his boasting about past sexual encounters. He was a sad little man who enjoyed taking advantage of vulnerable women and an experienced proprietor of whore houses. He laughed when informing me about how officials of the Social Department of the Interior Ministry had proposed legalizing prostitution and setting up brothels, calling them 'morality houses', as a way to manage the trade and control the spread of HIV.

I had been told about the sexual exploitation of women and girls in Iran by my feminist friends in Esfahan. They claimed that many mullahs and officials are involved in the inhumane and illegal trade of vulnerable females. For example, following the earthquake in Bam orphaned girls were kidnapped and taken to a known slave market in Tehran where Iranian and foreign traders meet. Women have reported that in order to have a judge approve a divorce they have to have sex with him. Women who are arrested for prostitution say they must have sex with the arresting officer. I was struggling to fully accept these 'supposed truths,' as I had been treated with such unending hospitality and kindness. Although I felt on the surface the country instils respect and tolerance, it wasn't difficult to believe that exploitation and abuse exists.

I feel similarly about Islam. When taken in its truest form it is a code to be revered. However, as is evident from the number of diverse people I have met, Islam is interpreted in an infinite number of ways, causing controversy, bitterness and confusion. People often use the word of Allah to promote their own agenda while labelling those who question their motives as racist or anti-Muslim. Honest honourable

Muslims have implored me not to label certain individuals, or whole other sects as Muslim because of their differing views but I feel I am in no position to judge who can and cannot claim a certain faith.

The Kurd puffed out his chest and stated with alleged benevolence that because of the high unemployment rate of young women he was providing them with a means by which to become independent. It was common for young women to turn to prostitution after running away from abusive arranged marriages. I criticized his attitude but he retorted that even two members of the Iranian national football squad were recently caught in a brothel. He pleaded with me to accompany him to a local establishment free of charge, where he claimed the women were so high on heroine they would happily do whatever debauched acts a man could think of.

13

Shadows in Uniform

Thankfully I avoided all security checks in the early morning and cycled towards the border through wilderness of blood red mountains disrupting flat desert. Pickup trucks piled high with diesel canisters plied the route bringing in fuel from Pakistan to sell illegally. Even though fuel is cheap in Iran its consumption is restricted, forcing people to buy on the black market.

The border was negotiated easily and I delighted in being able to talk freely in English to money changers who tried to rip me off. As I made my way towards town a police vehicle pulled alongside and invited me to take a free bus ride to Quetta. I declined. They insisted. I leaned in to greet the Superior officer with a kiss, as had been expected of me for the past month, but he withdrew leaving me extremely embarrassed. He took his pistol from his belt in case I made another attempt at physical affection. I knew it was probable that I would have to bus it through this section of Pakistan but only gave in after an exasperating episode of arguments. I was manhandled onto a bus but assured I would be allowed to continue alone from Quetta.

My bike perched on the roof and I sat down next to a scrawny man who looked as if he had been dragged through the desert by one of the roaming camels. The bus was decorated in extravagant designs and the driver sped as if he were carrying thirty two female passengers in labour. The road was single lane and the bus lurched over rough ground, passing battered old cars and engulfing villages in clouds of dust. The horn was a musical tune which blasted out at every opportunity, deafening all in the vicinity. Men covered their faces with checkered black and white cloths and rode motorbikes through the sand with rifles over their shoulders.

We stopped abruptly at a cluster of huts. All the men scampered around the back to relieve themselves in an open field. I tagged along, unzipped and waited for the moment of release. The smell of rotting faeces made me retch. I looked to my side to see twenty men, all wearing knee length baggy shirt like kurtas, crouched low to the ground and staring up at me with quizzical expressions. Whichever direction I pointed I felt uneasy as men squatted and splashed their backsides from little jugs of water.

I gave up, retreated to the eating area and sat on a mat next to a big bearded man with bright red hennaed hair, signifying his recent trip to the holy city of Mecca. He sat in an upright posture, his heavy paunch inflating and deflating. He encouraged me to eat, slapping lamb chunks onto my plate as I swatted clouds of flies. People didn't seem to notice and sat as docile as cows with flies covering their arms and ears.

'What do you think of our Mr President Musharraf?' He asked, eyeing me seriously.

All I knew about him was that he was an ally of America and equally loved and hated throughout the country.

'He has a nice moustache,' cringing at my attempt at humour.

'To call Musharraf a dog would be an insult to dogs,' he responded, searching the crowd for a confrontation.

Another man chirped, 'I believe he should be hanged twice. Once for disrespecting our religion and twice for associating with the devil.'

I answered all other questions with, 'Tawakkaltu ala-Allah' (In God we trust) or 'Inshallah.'

I was invited to stay the night with Najeeb, a young man returning from Iran where he studied, to visit his family in Quetta. His oriental looking face was broad with high cheek bones and a fair complexion. He was inquisitive but guarded with his answers as if embarrassed about the truth. We made our way through dark streets in the back of

Curious Companions

a truck accompanied by his tutor Ali who was also on his way home to Lahore.

We lounged in Najeeb's small but tidy room and discussed religion. Ali had an air of sophistication, was an extremely intelligent individual and a good example of the compassion and acceptance of even some of the most faithful of Islamic scholars. He had been studying in Qom, the Iranian Islamic centre for learning, for the past sixteen years and his understanding of Christianity was far greater than my own. He wore his beard neatly trimmed and his shirt crisply ironed. He was enthusiastic to increase my understanding of his most sacred religion and told me about his cherished young wife. Najeeb sat quietly respectful in front of his elder.

I was awoken by stomach pains. I had not been allowed to greet Najeeb's mother or sisters and knew they were all asleep on the floor of the main living room. I fumbled with the door lock and negotiated my way, tiptoeing over sleeping bodies to the bathroom. My stomach protested over an agonizing two hours of cramps and sweating palpitations. I suffocated my cries of agony in a towel and fell asleep curled up on the cool concrete floor.

For two days I wore a path between the bedroom and the bathroom. Every time I appeared his sisters and mother wrapped their shawls around their heads and scuttled off to hide in the kitchen. They observed strict purdah where women are secluded from unrelated male company. I felt bad for my intrusions but was unable to apologize. I felt like a leper. Najeeb was kind but spent most of his time out visiting friends. He arrived back at intervals to cajole me into leaving bed but all I could think about was not fainting, throwing up or soiling my trousers.

On the third morning we sat on a bridge with three friends and chatted in the first rays of sunlight. All wore battered Nike trainers along with their fawn salwar kameez. They appeared to be clean shaven as only a handful of facial hairs disrupted their smooth skin. Ruddy faced school kids ran after puppies. Young girls wore matching light blue flowing shawls, their pretty little faces peeking out from under white head scarves. We clung to motorbikes and raced each other through crowded streets and out into the open countryside. We played checkers under the shade of trees and munched on greasy *pakoras*. I was asked about the myth of sex education in schools in the West. They thought it hilarious, believing pupils were taught how to be good at sex. They were disappointed to hear about classes on preventing the spread of diseases and sexual responsibility.

Although hesitant, Najeeb began to confide in me his painful history. Ten years before when his Hazara people were being persecuted by the Sunni Taliban, his family had fled their homeland in Afghanistan to Pakistan. His ancestors he claimed were colonists from Mongolia who had conquered the isolated highlands of Afghanistan with Genghis Khan. He cared little for what country I might label him from but was truly proud of his battle hardened Hazara origins.

The guys told me their dreams of escaping to Australia on an illegal boat due to their constant fears of suicide bombers in their adopted home. Since the US invasion of Afghanistan, the Taliban have also fled their country resulting in Quetta having a tense atmosphere as the two warring peoples live alongside each other in a foreign land. They felt intimidated and cynical. One of the quieter guys lifted up his shirt to reveal a disfigured chest and scars covering his torso. He had been kidnapped and tortured by the Taliban three years before but had managed to escape. He thanked God to be alive but his anger would never leave his bitter face. They had little idea about geography and debated the pros and cons of visiting the other well known safe haven of Italy on the way to their new lives in Australia. They believed happiness and prosperity were only possible somewhere else. I agonized over their idea of Eurotopia.

Hungry goats with long beards loitered, groups of men with matching beards strolled along the riverside staring as we ducked ourselves into the freezing river. My friends recognized many as Taliban and the confrontational looks made everyone anxious.

We visited the house of Sadat, a chubby vivacious character, who told me how the Taliban 'dogs' targeted the Hazara with particular brutality due to their Shia faith. He put on footage from illegal cds showing Hazara men being beheaded by the Taliban. A shirtless man with hands tied behind his back and wearing a blindfold knelt before the camera. A foot long knife slashed his throat. His body struggled

Curious Companions

and shuddered, blood squirted from the neck onto the parched ground. The triumphant man standing behind held the head aloft. The blindfold came lose, the eyes looking startled. His executioners cheered and brought out another victim for slaughter.

My friends became understandably distraught. They possessed a silent rage common with groups on the margins of society. Many had lost fathers, brothers or friends. I felt inadequate with my sympathies as some began to cry while others cursed incessantly.

The bike felt unstable, my body lethargic. The traffic was manic, a nerve shredding high. Vehicles fought for every possible inch, looking no further than the bumper ahead. No one was actively hostile, everyone was just trying to get to the same place at the same time. No consideration, no hard feelings. People seemed exhilarated by the intensity of life. Men on scooters invited me to their homes, traffic police requested bribes. I ignored the world.

I was deep in thought as the factories, car mechanics and *chai* shops slowly withdrew leaving me alone in the desert. Chimneys of brick making factories pumped out smoke on the horizon. I met the Baluchistan cycling team who implored me not to continue and return with them to Quetta. They were a comical bunch of guys with ill-fitting jerseys.

Trucks slowed to observe me, bedecked in vibrant colours, shimmering attachments, chrome ornaments, mirrors, portraits; the personification of the poor man's pride. They were piled high with firewood, large copper pots, bales of straw, blankets, livestock and their owners perched on top. These nomads were moving from the hot plains to the more temperate hills and I yearned to go with them. Their encampments dotted the outskirts of towns, flimsy homemade tents of palm matting surrounded by piles of drying dung and people squatting beside campfires. The women wore large earrings, nose rings, silver bracelets and necklaces, had permanent frowns and weather beaten faces. The children had hair like straw, huge smiles and seemed oblivious to their hardship.

The road swooped through a timeless village clinging to the hillside. A checkpoint signalled for me to stop. My legs instinctively quickened the pace but I slammed on the brakes as a police car pulled out blocking my path. I was led into the dimly lit confines of a hut with great fanfare. The sub-inspector had the brains of a sheep and introduced himself as Zahir. His eyes were blank, his movements laborious. We discussed how I had come to be there in the mountains of Baluchistan. He did not believe me. Once again I was facing the prospect of being driven. He explained how the surrounding areas had always been under tribal rule but now the army had imposed government law. This had understandably caused problems within the community resulting in fighting in the mountains. Three 'rebels' had been killed two days before as they attempted an ambush on a military post nearby. I had no choice but to accept their imposed invitation to sleep at the checkpoint.

My sexual history was of paramount importance to the assembled posse of law enforcement. I was unable to change the direction of the conversation.

'How many girls you fuck sir?' Asked an impish man, smiling at me expectantly.

'Three.' I thought it better not to encourage them but alas the commotion and applause took a few minutes to die down.

'And they were virgins?' Zahir asked, taking over and hushing the assembly.

'One was and the other two were not.' I was afraid of reinforcing the stereotypical opinion that all Western girls act like sluts and will shag any man, anytime, anyplace.

'Ah I think virgin was good no? Other girls were prostitutes. How much you pay?' He looked at his comrades in search of admiration for his command of a foreign language.

'They were all good but no I did not pay. In my country if you are in a relationship with a girl it is considered ok to have sex.'

I wanted to escape but knew I could not stem the rising flurry of excitement.

Curious Companions

'Virgin good sir. Small,' clenching a fist.

'You fuck virgin more one time?'

'What age she?'

'Young is good. Small.'

'How much wife cost?'

'Free wow. You lucky man.'

'My brother fuck donkey.'

'My father fuck my mother.'

'No. My father fuck your donkey mother.'

Half of the men were married but the others like Zahir, had no sexual experience and asked questions like inquisitive adolescent boys. He repeated my answers, congratulating me as if I were the first man to have ever overcome the obstacle of sexual intercourse.

'Girls are evil when they drink alcohol sir. You fuck girl that evil?' He was an ignorant, exceptionally sexist man and I felt for the woman who would be forced to tolerate him in the future. I thought it probably better that he marry the permissible four wives for at least they would be able to share the burden.

The sub-inspector's bald assistant was a tanned replica of *Keith Woods* and sat in the back of the pickup with rifle at the ready as we bumped along the rutted road towards Mach. We drove over a riverbed looking up at a huge contorted bridge which had collapsed during the previous monsoon. Zahir ordered the driver to send text messages on his mobile phone even though he was precariously negotiating between thundering lorries and a sheer drop into a canyon. He enjoyed asserting his authority at every opportunity.

Mach is a scraggy market town with muddy streets and impoverished inhabitants. Rubbish was piled high in the square and raw sewage lay stagnant in the gutter. Men with large beards and sparkling hats crowded the windows zombie style. Some knocked on the glass to draw my attention. We got stuck in the melee and Muhammad Woods had to threaten people to move, pointing his rifle in their distraught faces.

We sat in a squalid teahouse. The filth stained walls displayed an abstract design of browns and greys, the floor was a slushy mess of mud, sawdust and broken concrete and the air was thick with flies. In pranced Zahir's cousin. He was a handsome fifty two year old and possessed a certain panache. He had married his wife ten years previously but now at twenty four she was apparently useless.

'She give me four children. Only one boy. She is a bad wife. She old and not good in bed.'

Zahir commiserated by patting him on the back.

'Now I will take new wife. She is daughter of man in my village.' He slapped my leg and squeezed my knee.

I knew daughters were often considered a moral and financial burden on families and were regularly married off as early as was possible.

'Can I ask what your wife will think?' I knew the answer but felt obliged to confront him.

He frowned and withdrew his hand. 'I no care my wife think. She is MY wife. She do what I say. I am tribal. I am King. She only woman. She not do what I say I kill her no problem.' He threw his hands in the air, puffed out his chest and smacked the table.

Zahir calmed him by relating my sexual history which seemed to gain me approval.

'I took my wife for get children and now I want love marriage,' he continued.

I wondered how this 'love' had developed in a society which strictly forbids any contact between the opposite sexes outside of the immediate family. 'So you love this woman?' I asked timidly.

'Yes she beautiful woman. I love her. She not woman. She twelve. She small. She thirteen when we marry. I love her.'

Zahir grinned and made a fist, his cousin looked smug.

They continued to babble about the idiosyncrasies of womanhood and I heard them out with silent misgivings. It was quite obvious this was a sex marriage in the making. I was mourning the life of an innocent twelve year old girl who would live her life under this callous man's absolute control, her life damned due to her untarnished chastity.

Three haggard looking men sat silently in the corner. Even this dump looked too stylish for them. Hardened blood caked one's face, another's arm and stained all of their tattered clothes. One had a humorously half bald head with long straggly streaks of hair knotted together at the sides. They spat on the floor in turns and stared at us with vacant expressions.

On our way back to the barracks Zahir began to coerce me into getting him an Irish visa. As we were now 'brothers' it was apparently my duty. I said I would try but that visas are very difficult to come by. He insulted me then asked how much a woman would cost. I explained the system of marriage proposal which he found ludicrous.

'You tell a man to give me his daughter. I give him money no problem. I make good money as sub-inspector in Irish. She no have beautiful. Big girl no problem,' he said impersonating a woman with large breasts.

He refused to believe that women had a choice of whom they wanted to marry and that it was not the decision of their father.

'I love her. I love sex with her like you my brother.'

I gave up my attempt at cultural education and feigned sleep. I hoped to wake up somewhere else. It was two a.m.

For breakfast we crouched around the hut listening to the crackle of Zahir's radio. We munched on a juicy watermelon that had been commandeered as toll. The other men were congenial and patient as they obeyed their pathetic excuse for a superior officer. I was eager to say goodbye but was forced into the pickup once again to visit the military barracks. No doubt Zahir was keen to show off his new foreign accomplice.

We drove up a dirt track and were greeted by a group of thirty army personnel. We went through an endless spiel of introductions and greetings then stood around the doorway saying 'come, please,' to one another. I sat down and let them deal with the question of the group's status. I was given the privileged position furthest away from the door, seated next to an RAF officer and the lieutenant colonel on one side and the insufferable sub-inspector on the other. A large feast of snacks was presented. There was a carnival atmosphere as all piled into the hut to listen to me speak on Western thought. I explained my opinion that men use different religions to speak to God, just as we use different languages to talk to one another. 'La ilaha illallah' (There is no God but God), I said, not sure if I was making any sense.

Several were fair skinned with blue eyes and fingered prayer beads as they observed me intently. Others sat fidgeting with their undeveloped moustaches. The beefy chef amused everyone with his laugh, 'ark ark ark, ark ark ark.'

In another shed I admired their weaponry. Shelves were packed full of grenades, pistols, rifles and rocket launchers. I admitted to having never shot a rifle before which caused outrage and several guns of different shapes and sizes were thrust into my arms. I smiled and cradled one unsure what to do. The lieutenant colonel took me gruffly by the arm and led me to a rise where he cocked the gun, aimed at the hillside half a kilometre away and pulled the trigger. A cloud of dust rose in the distance and my ears rang loudly. I looked around to see everyone with their fingers in their ears. He giggled and told me, 'I will show you how to kill.'

I was keen on using the weapon but not so sure about the homicide part. The bullet clanked into place, I placed the butt to my shoulder, peered through the sight aiming at a non-descript rock and squeezed the trigger. My ears rang louder. Men's faces looked as if they were cheering but all was silent except the ringing. I was hugged and back slapped but my request to sample the rocket launcher was denied.

I promised to send the lads at the checkpost their two most requested items, a box of viagra and 'pictures of woman no clothes.' This was received as the best news all year and they thanked Allah for sending them this Irish purveyor of porn.

I cycled through steep sided mountains desperately trying to ignore the police car following me and beseeching me to take a lift. I agreed it would be a lot easier, faster and cheaper but I remained resolute that I was going to cycle. The sun shone brightly. I was stopped at the next checkpoint by a Saddam Hussain look-a-like with a fearsome moustache. He had a flabby face and watery eyes and enquired politely about the health of every member of my family, then ordered me off my bike and the infuriating process of negotiation continued. To my surprise a bright yellow truck pulled over displaying the words, 'Show Your Hope'. I considered it a good sign.

Martin was an ex-roadie who had turned to art as an alternative to saving his soul. The Dutch eccentric had accumulated paintings by over fifty artists on the subject of Hope, bought an old fire engine and decided to drive to India. He had taken a similar route to me since leaving Amsterdam three weeks before. Along with the seven foot tall Bart and his five foot wife Beatrice, they had stopped at cities along the route and displayed the exhibition. They used galleries when available but sometimes simply parked the bus and stuck the Velcro backed paintings to its flanks. Martin was a passionate storyteller and related the stories of the artist's portrayal of Hope, presumably creating a positive atmosphere. They told me how people often didn't understand what the purpose of the performance was but appreciated them for coming to their country in a great yellow bus. I enjoyed their many stories before departing in Jacobabad. I promised to see their show once I arrived in India.

As I loaded the bike the next morning a police truck arrived and marked the beginning of an infuriating six days. They refused to let me cycle alone so I told them if they cared to follow then that was their prerogative. They looked at each other, confused by why I chose to battle the heat and rutted roads when they were offering me a lift gratis. I was passed down the line from one police mobile unit to another every fifteen kilometres. They habitually drove alongside gesticulating to jump in and chill out. I tried to ignore them and shouted that I was having the time of my life. It was forty two degrees. My face and lungs burnt, the road a shimmering haze, the wind an overheated hairdryer on full blast. The water in my drinking bottle was too hot to drink so I stopped regularly at chai stalls to down cold bottles of pepsi alongside inquisitive locals under the watchful eye of my escort.

'It is our duty to protect you kind sir,' I was told repeatedly.

I questioned, 'from whom?' And received a shrug. 'I know Baluchistan is dangerous but this area is not dangerous is it?'

'No sir not dangerous.'

'So why do I need protection?'

'Because it is our duty sir.'

The police were kind and congenial but I felt like an unwelcome wedding guest who everyone expected to cause trouble at any second. Arriving at hotels after long days in the saddle the police sat outside my door and refused to let me leave. I pleaded to go explore the town but was told it was 'too dangerous'. I wrote long impossible shopping lists for my body guards to buy and told them I would complain unless every item was found. I felt bitter about losing my freedom and being removed from the country I was so keen to experience.

One night I kicked up such a fuss that the Inspector was summoned. He shifted uncomfortably on the small bed opposite me, sipping a fizzy drink and ignoring my insolence having not bothered to wear more than my boxer shorts in his Excellency's presence. His manner was authoritative without being intimidating. He spoke in a calm polite way while brushing his gelled hair across the top of his bald scalp with his hand, reminding me of *Jackie Healy Rae*. I told him I had been invited to see his wonderful country but that I was being held prisoner. He leaned forward, his head bowed, indicating unusually that he listened as much as he commanded. I explained I didn't want or need an escort for now in Punjab there was no danger to me. He again repeated the 'duty' line so I raised my voice telling the head of the police that his reasoning was idiotic and made no sense. He looked at his assistant and said in a composed way that he would tell me the truth. I hadn't expected there was another 'truth' but welcomed it nonetheless.

'You must understand sir that our great country of Pakistan is at war. A war that has lasted a long time with India our most hated enemy. You sir have been to that country several times and our intelligence service has ordered for you to be under police escort at all times during your stay in our great country.'

I laughed at the accusations but began to feel uncomfortable about my inappropriate attire. 'I am Irish sir. I am unconcerned with the grievances between your country and India. While in that country I was given the freedom to explore, to meet ordinary people, to experience the lives of those of different religions, to make friends. But here I am treated like a criminal.'

I felt bad for talking ill of the gentleman's beloved country but needed to do all I could to persuade him that I was not an international spy but an Irishman who went for a cycle ride.

Curious Companions

'Please do not leave the hotel until morning sir. You are very beautiful and the girls will be looking at you.'

He proceeded to pay for my stay despite my protests.

A wedding party sang and beat drums in the back of a tractor trailer. They waved and cheered as I ambled by. I noticed several stunningly beautiful girls amongst the crowd, smooth skin taut over defined cheek bones. They wore their finest saris, huddled together with legs drawn up close. My escort pulled up close to ward off two friendly guys on a motorbike. The traffic became heavy and the siren was put on as the police vehicle struggled to keep up as I dodged bullock carts and cyclists carrying huge bundles of hay. I ate bean curry with chapattis while my sentries stood over me inspecting everyone as if an assassination attempt was imminent.

The uniforms lay on the hotel bed tickling each other and flicking channels on the TV. I was in no mood for their immature carry-on so told them to find somewhere else to sleep and locked the door to sulking faces. I knew they were only obeying orders but resented their presence. Of course I was acting like the unappreciative rich white kid they all presumed me to be.

Tractors pulled impossibly wide loads of sugarcane and I sat with some young boys, munched on the stalks and slept for an hour on a rope bed beside a fertilizer plant. I cycled past golden fields of corn glistening in the afternoon sunlight. Heads of men popped up to watch me pass. Women with dazzlingly colourful saris were bent double gathering the precious crop. Donkeys scratched themselves as they waited patiently for their next load. At one stop I was joined by my bodyguards. They wore tight t-shirts that signified they were part of the country's Elite Force. By their bulging bellies I guessed they hadn't seen action for a while. They were instantly charming and were in awe of my trip. I received hugs all around as I remounted to continue.

I paused at a canal where a large herd of goats was being watered. I stomped up the dry mud slope ignoring the shouts of officers behind

Curious Companions

me. I hurled myself into the brown water desperate to rid myself of my shadows. The cool water was orgasmic, rushing over my overheated body. I looked up at distressed men in uniforms contemplating whether I was worth saving. The shepherds looked amused, the sheep thought I was nuts. I drifted in the current, the overweight police plodding after me. I lay on the road drying off, trying to ignore everyone's compliments and polite best wishes. I wanted to be angry at them but their goodwill overcame my ignorance.

14

Body, Mind and Soul

Lahore is a big city. I knew it had a painful history. Wraith-like figures stood frozen in the street, invisible to humanity. Wilting skin draped over naked bones and eyes full of terror.

Having been unable to secure an Indian visa in Iran I was now faced with having to travel north to Islamabad. The previous two weeks had been a struggle, mentally and physically. I was fraught by the idea of a lengthy detour with more babysitting law enforcement. I locked my bike in a compound with ancient rusted and battered bicycles and knew it was probably fifty-fifty whether it would be there on my return. I hopped joyfully onto a train.

Captain Ahmad was a handsome, clean cut and arrogant twenty six year old. He bought me snacks and claimed he had broken so many girl's hearts. He tried to impress me with his knowledge of English football but merely named the world's top ten players. I questioned him about the Taliban taking refuge in the lawless tribal areas of Pakistan and he retorted that I should learn more about religion before condemning it. Two members of the Pakistan Under Nineteen Cricket Team told me about a suicide bomb in Karachi.

The taxi driver pretended not to speak English until we arrived at a hotel where he proceeded to justify charging me double because of being blessed with so many children. At the Diplomatic Enclave I filled out forms to check in my bag and others to board a bus. The queue was as long as a *St. Patrick's Day* parade. An obnoxious, obese man told me to move aside, sticking his Press identity card in my face. A kind doctor on his way to Delhi for a conference on AIDs told the journalist to move back and go on a diet. The invisible face behind the scratched glass told me the visa would take at least seven working days. The fat man's belly prodded me from behind. I felt peeved.

At a park I was summoned to play cricket. There must have been fifteen groups of boys and men of all ages standing around looking at each other with an occasional flurry of excitement. Before I could figure out who was doing what they had become immobile once again. I held the bat tightly while trying to make out the bowler against the sun's glare. I saw him run in my direction. There was cheering. I enquired what happened. Nobody seemed to know. Everyone stood around content.

I was transferred to another game. The players seemed smaller. I waited with hands in pockets in the corner of the park by overgrown bushes where a couple were hiding from curious onlookers. They too resented my presence. He stroked her hand, she played with her mobile. After a while I sat down and watched giant ants crawl up my leg. There was shouting so I stood up again to see the ball bounce on the rock hard earth in front of me. I plucked it out of the air with a catch that would have made *Dara O'Shea* proud, ran towards the sticks and hurled it as hard as I could at the batsman. The big eyed kid dropped the bat and collapsed to the dust with a whimper. All my life I have gotten into trouble for throwing things. I guess now's an appropriate time to apologize to my neighbours.

Having been forcibly retired, I ate *samosas* in a crowded canteen. I ignored the suspicious looks from all around and drew a sketch of a sleeping man curled up ontop of a wall. Two gruff teenagers sat across the table from me, slapping their plastic chairs down loudly. Their middle-aged friend had converging eyes and stood behind caressing their shoulders. They spat brown tobacco stained saliva on the greasy floor.

'I'm sorry I can't be on your cricket team today my friends. I'm out in it man for two thousand and sixty divided by four under a run of ninety to eighty four wickets all inside it.' I know nothing about cricket and missed talking about *pucking a sliotar*.

They were not amused. One shifted his prayer hat to the side as if it made him look cooler.

'Who you are?' Asked the skinny dude with a scowl.

'The name's Jake. How are ya man?'

'Where is your God?'

Ah feck it, I thought, just when I was enjoying my day along comes another religious condemnation.

'He is at home watching *Glenroe*.' For the first time in my life I too wished I was watching it. The world works in mysterious ways.

'You afraid to die because you have no God.'

'Check please,' I said to the dribbling ruffian who had brought my appetizer. 'I believe life is a gift and should not be wasted. Every human being has a right to live however he or she chooses as long as it doesn't harm the lives of others. Would you like a sticker?'

He translated for his friend and asked me what a 'shikkar' was.

I had carried a sheet of small shamrock stickers to distribute as an Irish token of friendship and they had successfully broken many awkward silences. Emilio's sock gloves in London, the nun's habit in France, the war veteran's whiskey bottle in Germany, Elena's headboard in Romania, Asra's teddy in Turkey, Ozgur's samurai sword in Ankara, several went to the Michael Jackson dancing kids, the gay baker's coffee table, the teenager's motorbike in Malayer, the young shepherd's hut, Mimi's headscarf, a concrete tunnel in an Iranian desert, the back of a bus seat in Baluchistan and the rifle of my favourite policeman in Southern Pakistan had all been christened with one. Sharing the love I thought.

I asked to see his prayer hat and stuck the little green leafed label next to an intricate design of beads and sequins. He carefully replaced it on his head with the shamrock at the front and looked at his friend who nodded in approval.

'I will die for my God. My father, my brother kill infidels. I will be martyr for my jihad.' He spat between my feet.

I represented a religion and a culture that those guys were programmed to detest. Ali had taught me that true Islam is achieved by attempting to live a pure life in the exterior world. This requires a constant 'struggle in the way of Allah.' Fight against temptation and strive for the ideals of Islam. This incessant personal struggle for goodness is the true meaning of the word jihad, as I understand it, not the common misinterpretation of the slaughter of 'unbelievers' in the name of Allah.

'May God protect your home and your family,' I said in Arabic, while thrusting a bill into the waiter's hand and paying everyone's check.

Thankfully they did not follow.

I lay on the bed staring at the rotating fan. It stopped. I anticipated a cloud of mosquitoes. It began again. I wiped sweat from my forehead and pulled the blanket over my shivering corpse. It stopped again. I was suffering from fever. My back felt as if I had been snuggled by an elephant. I couldn't keep my legs still which had apparently taken me on a marathon and then been pummelled by iron rods without me ever realizing it.

'Every human heartbeat is a universe of possibility.' My bag lay dormant on the floor with my favourite quotation inscribed on it. How stupid I thought.

There were footsteps on a wooden floor and an echo of voices. I swallowed a handful of painkillers. I threw them up on my pillow. I took another handful and woke up two days later with samosa in my hair.

The cricket teams in the park were still standing around looking at their hands. I caught an eleven seater with eighteen others to Murree. I was bored of the big city and thought a few days in the cool mountain air would do my health good. Giant billboards mingled with lush forests. My seatmate slept with his head on my shoulder as we careened around never ending bends. Houses clung to the hillside and a new highway bisected the green with a light brown scar.

An ensemble of hotel touts, porters, shoe shiners, carpet sellers, flocks of grim looking Pakistani tourists and smiling beggars wrestled for supremacy and received my bleary eyed disregard. I had come to this hill station in search of peace and privacy and my cynical mind objected to others having the same intention. Wandering the steep cobbled streets, I ducked low under washing lines and was pulled by the hand of a grubby little boy into a shack made from rusted tin and plastic sheeting. Stooping low to enter the dark interior I was greeted by his father who sat praying in silence. My little buddy fetched a tin mug of pale brown water which I pretended to drink with expressions of delight. I thought about what prospects the future could possibly hold for this little munchkin. He sat by my side, toyed with my watch and held my finger with adorably tiny hands. We both became distraught when I eventually decided I must continue before it became too dark.

The sun peered through the morning mist as I sat on a wall overlooking the main street along with twenty or so men wearing shabby turbans and reading the morning papers. I chatted to similarly bored shopkeepers and mechanics and could not rid myself of the feeling of time lost. I craved a pint. I had been as sober as a potato for over a month. I thought the mosque was probably a good place to visit. A man chastised me for taking a photo of a stray cat. He told me it was forbidden to take photos inside or outside mosques. He claimed it was not due to religious conservativeness or intrusion but that 'people' had graphically manipulated photographs of mosques to portray a negative image of Islam and discredit his precious religion.

The reactions my camera received over the months had been divided. Some people were enamoured, feeling honoured that I would go to the trouble of taking their photo. The joy on their faces due to my simple and selfish act of preserving my memories was priceless. I chose, however, to keep my camera hidden away just as often. Some felt offended and understandably resented being used as a form of tourist memorabilia. Others thought it was against their religious beliefs but invariably didn't know why. Many were shy or even scared by my strange manoeuvring for a better position. I captured individuals I would prefer to forget while other kind faces will never fade in my memory.

Eventually arriving back in Lahore with visa tucked away, I gratefully collected my safely guarded bike. I mounted my faithful steed for what was to be the final leg of the trip. Bullock carts, dogs, fruit carts, frail looking men carrying large bundles of wood, cloth or cardboard, buses, *cycle rickshaws*, scooters and tiny overloaded donkeys jostled for space. Towns were swept by dust storms and a crippled beggar pleaded with me for change. His legs were twisted under his shrivelled body and he dragged himself along on a makeshift skateboard. I gave him money and he looked skyward declaring, 'Allah-u-Akbar' (God is great). Talk about looking on the bright side of life.

At the Wagha border, television station trucks, cameramen and reporters dotted the parking area. According to a policeman the family of an Indian 'terrorist' had been allowed to visit their loved one before his imminent execution. They were apparently returning home that day creating a great commotion. I showed my passport to the last Pakistani guard, walked two metres and showed it to an Indian who could have passed for his twin brother. He welcomed me and shot a glance over my shoulder at his enemy. I freewheeled past a wall of photographers who chatted excitedly. One bored guy took my photo.

Luggagewallas sat in the shade of giant poplar and eucalyptus trees and I joined them. I delighted in seeing their waggling heads. I made a comment, all heads waggled. They grunted in agreement, I joined in. They were sad to hear about the impending execution.

Old Sikh men with magnificent long beards and brightly coloured and perfectly formed turbans cycled along with an air of pride. A beautiful girl with flowing black hair and pink sari fluttering in the breeze waited for her bus and I nearly crashed as I passed. Adorable school girls wearing matching red socks and ribbons in their hair poured out of school. Little boys wore red turbans and sang happily.

Curious Companions

A poor man cycling a rickshaw piled high with all his worldly possessions creaked by. I revelled in the freedom after the previous few weeks of confrontation with the authorities.

In Amritsar I wasted little time negotiating the choked streets and headed straight to the Golden Temple. This most famous Sikh temple, or gurdwara, provides hospitality for all races and creeds. I was given a hard wood bed in the foreigner's dormitory and greeted a nervous looking Korean couple. The courtyard was packed with hundreds of Indian families sprawled on the concrete floor. Men washed themselves in the open communal showers, their hair hung down their backs and they wore cloth tied in a knot as underwear.

I secured a piece of orange cloth like a bandana to my head and went to explore the temple complex. I wondered why the world views Muslim women's headscarves with such disdain while male Sikh turbans are generally revered. I tiptoed through the shallow pond, awkwardly copying all those around me who bent to touch the ground at the entrance. The inner lake sparkled. It was surrounded by a three storey white complex of intricate design where people sheltered under archways. The smooth marble felt comforting under my bare feet. The small golden temple stood alone in the middle of the lake, reached by a busy narrow walkway. Thousands of pilgrims walked arm in arm around the perimeters, laughing and cajoling each other to stand for photos with foreigners.

The place exuded contentment, the atmosphere of a *Fair Day* back home. I sat in the shade of the archway with legs crossed to prevent insult with the soles of my feet. Groups hovered by the lake's edge, several dipping themselves in the holy water for their daily cleansing. I stole glances at teenage girls who strutted as if on a runway. My eyes were greedy having been in a no-woman zone for the previous eighty days. I had to remind myself to reel in my tongue and stop staring. Small kids came to chat and have their photos taken wearing my sunglasses. They were so proud of their turbans but knew nothing of animosity towards those without. The soothing *kirtan* chant of a *guru* filled the air. The temple shone in the last rays of the day. I had reached India.

My fever resurfaced that night. I cursed my vulnerable body and queued alongside jibbering old men for the bathrooms. I clung to the wall, my weak legs unable to support my shivering body. Horrific noises emanated from the stalls. Men abandoned the queue system. I bent double in pain. Men pushed. I concentrated on breathing. I thought there was going to be a riot when a hand guided me into a cubicle just in time. It was three a.m. I staggered through the courtyard, tripping over sleeping curled up bodies. The world spun, I hallucinated as if on some kind of new psychedelic drug. I forgot where I was. I repeated my journey.

After a few fitful hours of sleep I was awakened by two extremely cheerful, delighted to be alive, loving the world, on happy pills, Americans. I managed to half open my diseased looking eyes.

'Hey man, fantastic day outside man. There's a wicked lake for swimming and these dudes give you free food. As much as you want. Come on man get up and let's go party.'

I wished it was a nightmare but it continued relentlessly for two straight days. They made a friend from Germany who refused to talk and had dreadlocks down to his ass which he regularly displayed, also being averse to clothing. Apparently he had been in India for two years living off the goodwill of the people. He was idolized by the dudes. I despised him. I despised the world.

The antibiotics eventually made me feel human again so I decided to leave my by now rather homely abode. The communal kitchen was a hive of activity. I accepted a small tin bowl and lined up on a mat next to a daydreaming woman. Her head flopped to the side and her body swayed. Men walked around the aisles of hundreds of hungry pilgrims filling bowls with various types of vegetable dishes. I gratefully received rice. Two young tattered blonde girls looked at me through a mass of faces. I pretended not to see them. I didn't understand the concept of coming to India and trying to look as old and dishevelled as was humanly possible.

I thanked the smiling little man who collected my bowl.

'Come, come,' he said, so I followed him into the kitchen. There was pandemonium.

'Good time come visit. Is quiet,' throwing the stack of bowls into a cauldron of dirty water. 'Now you work. Yes?'

'Yes.'

'What is your good name sir?'

'Jake.'

'*Achha* good Jake Washwalla.'

I sat on the floor and smiled at several people drenched wet from washing up. I timidly scrubbed. My neighbour laughed.

'Hey, I washed pots for a whole summer when I was your age in the five star Sheen Falls Hotel. Have you stayed there? It's a wonderful place. Fabulous views of Kenmare Bay, a lovely spa and a classy restaurant. Anyway, so please don't tell me how to do washing up if you don't mind.'

He looked suitably confused, I waggled my head, he copied, we laughed. He was about fifteen and wore a black turban tied in a tight bun. He squeaked in a high pitched girly voice, 'Will they give me job sir?' Quickening his pace, trying to impress.

'Maybe my friend, maybe,' knowing he didn't stand a chance against the *Poles*.

People carried large bundles of vegetables donated by visiting pilgrims. These in turn were chopped and cooked by others donating their time. Me, Mr Squeak and the others were responsible for the afters. I felt weak but enjoyed the company.

Along came a young guy who scowled as he was named, 'Achha good Kenneth Washwalla'.

From Kent, Kenneth had postponed his university studies and travelled to India against his parents' wishes.

'I doon't like the waye these people look at me you knooou. And who are theaay to tell me what too dooo. I mean I caan staay at any hotel you knooou. I think the waald revolves around understanding and compassion realay but I don't have to stay heaah if I don't wunt you knooou.'

'Yes that's right, they are damn nice people alright.'

'Exaactlah. You seee you understand maay. I think one must better oneself by seeing the truuuth that lies euonly within oneself.'

Ah Christ give me the 'Fuck em for a laugh' Americans any day.

Rebel against society's restraints on freedom of expression. Rebel against conforming to the West's idea of normality. Rebel against consumerism. Rebel against the constraints of formal marriage. Rebel against the laws on soft drugs. Rebel against the destruction of the environment. Rebel against chemicals. Rebel against anything or anybody who will listen because really all I want is ATTENTION.

I was only a few days from Delhi and I could not contain my desire to continue. I have always been slender or basically skinny, but over the next few days I lost more weight. My tyres made grooves in the melting tar but as long as I kept cycling the heat was bearable. Stopping for breaks was when sweat began cascading down my face. People stared from air-conditioned land cruisers. It was forty six degrees.

A group of *eunuchs* surrounded me at a restaurant. The men's faces were thickly painted. They wore multicoloured sparkling saris and the bangles on their wrists tinkled. One clapped loudly in my face and threatened to expose himself/herself unless I donated money. I replied, 'go ahead, I have one too.'

They screamed like spoilt adolescent girls and condemned me to bad luck forever.

'I thought you are now a woman?' I enquired, having thought these transsexual men had been castrated.

'But yes my name Matilda. I am woman with penis. Is nice. I show you,' she said in her now husky voice. Her cleanly shaven and dangerously pointed chin was showing an afternoon shadow.

'Ah no that's ok. You are very kind but no thank you,' I said, as I put a chunk of mutton into my mouth.

'Don't worry sir I no have balls. Balls makes mens crazy.'

I didn't argue as she seemed to know more about the topic than I did. I put a sticker on a stuffed bra. Red raw pimples decorated her shoulders. She asked me for a kiss, I declined.

At another pit stop I sheltered from the sun under a banyan tree. I ordered chai from a stall while two little barefooted girls plucked at my leg beseeching me for money. Their clothes were tattered but their eyes sparkled. They were experts at flattery and manipulation. Masters of survival.

A man slept on the rear seat of his cycle rickshaw, his mouth wide open like a gold fish, displaying a few rotten teeth alongside gold ones. I tried to take his photo but he woke up startled. We shook hands. I convinced him to trade vehicles for a couple of kilometres. He was reluctant at first to entrust me with his beloved rusting bucket of nails. He looked at my expensive steed with snobbish apathy and dismissed the gears as superfluous.

We mounted and with a push from a cheering crowd became engulfed by traffic. I had to push so hard to maintain momentum that I remained standing on the pedals while looking around to manoeuvre the awkward contraption and see if my companion had realized his good fortune and made his getaway. I urged passengers aboard but they simply looked at me with raised eyebrows. Thankfully as I pulled over with my feet skidding along the dusty road for lack of a brake, my smiling ally came running along with my bike at his side. He told me I was, 'the most good bicycle driver in India,' as apparently my bike had been remarkably uncooperative.

At a roundabout I observed the organised chaos. Motorbikes going in the wrong direction weaved between pedestrians who ignored protesting buses with young boys hanging perilously off the sides. A white bullock pulled a cart, its little owner crouched on a bed of scrap metal. A woman perched precariously on the rear stared at me, frozen like a statue. She had her knees pulled up to her chest, defining her space. Two currents of traffic came together, neither knowing nor caring who had the right of way. Horns blared, nobody cared. An invisible policeman stood in the middle waving, merely adding his whistle to the cacophony of noise. The woman remained paralysed.

The last day I was in high spirits, memorising the enticing sights, smells and sounds. I met a *sadhu* bedecked in orange robes and a matching *tilak* on his forehead. He sat half naked on the pavement in the lotus position, his long beard rested between his legs and his matted hair trailed on the ground behind him. He had denounced all his worldly possessions and travelled for over ten years in search of religious enlightenment. His head was obscured in a cloud as he smoked hash from a *chillum*. Getting stoned was his way of feeling closer to his God Shiva and it was his professional obligation to get wasted. He couldn't remember his name.

I wondered why there were no sadhus in Ireland. I know plenty of potential holy men – unemployed, lazy, hairy, wandering stoners. Personally I didn't envy his life of celibacy or the feats of yoga these men perform. Holding my hand above my head for years on end until the fingers shrivel to stumps or standing on one foot for an eternity, would I expect cloud my judgement and leave me more than a little pissed off with my creator.

I preferred my friend's approach of perpetually getting intoxicated with charras. The chillum was passed in my direction, it would have been rude to refuse and I didn't want yet another curse placed on me. Was it not my obligation to share this man's holy experience? Our glazed eyes locked together, stupefied. The world seemed a less complicated place. He was under the euphoria of religious pleasure. His bony hands clutched mine. A big dumb cow waddled over to join our primitive world.

I was very much like my stoned companion in a lot of ways. I couldn't specify exactly what I had learnt from my own adventure. I didn't find religious enlightenment nor did I realise the meaning of life, to be expected really as I hadn't actually been looking. I have however, proved irrevocably to myself that people should never be condemned because of their beliefs, opinions or the ways in which they chose to live. Preconceptions are usually wrong. People are habitually good. My life will be short. I am going to enjoy it.

'Saatch aur himmat' (Truth and Courage), I whispered, feeling whacked out of my mind.

'Hey baba, thank you,' said the smiling Indian rasta.

Curious Companions